Reading, Learning, Teaching
Kurt Vonnegut

confronting the Text, confronting the World

P. L. Thomas
General Editor

Vol. 2

PETER LANG
New York • Washington, D.C./Baltimore • Bern
Frankfurt am Main • Berlin • Brussels • Vienna • Oxford

P. L. Thomas

Reading, Learning, Teaching
Kurt Vonnegut

PETER LANG
New York • Washington, D.C./Baltimore • Bern
Frankfurt am Main • Berlin • Brussels • Vienna • Oxford

Library of Congress Cataloging-in-Publication Data
Thomas, P. L. (Paul Lee).
Reading, learning, teaching Kurt Vonnegut / P. L. Thomas.
p. cm. — (Confronting the text, confronting the world; v. 2)
Includes bibliographical references.
1. Vonnegut, Kurt—Criticism and interpretation.
2. Vonnegut, Kurt—Study and teaching. I. Title. II. Series.
PS3572.O5Z864   813'.54—dc22   2006012701
ISBN 978-0-8204-6337-7
ISSN 1556-8288

Bibliographic information published by **Die Deutsche Nationalbibliothek**.
Die Deutsche Nationalbibliothek lists this publication in the "Deutsche
Nationalbibliografie"; detailed bibliographic data are available
on the Internet at http://dnb.d-nb.de/.

Cover design by Lisa Barfield

The paper in this book meets the guidelines for permanence and durability
of the Committee on Production Guidelines for Book Longevity
of the Council of Library Resources.

© 2006, 2015 Peter Lang Publishing, Inc., New York
29 Broadway, 18th floor, New York, NY 10006
www.peterlang.com

All rights reserved.
Reprint or reproduction, even partially, in all forms such as microfilm,
xerography, microfiche, microcard, and offset strictly prohibited.

Printed in the United States of America

Table of Contents

Acknowledgment vii

Introduction: "So It Goes" 1

1   Kurt Vonnegut: You Can Take the Man out of the War,
    But You Can't Take the War out of the Man—Writer as
    Freethinker and Passivist 5
    Vonnegut as Fact and Fiction—The Life of a Writer 6
    The Works of Vonnegut 9
    Thoughts of a Freethinker—Themes and Concerns in
        Vonnegut's Work 19
    Craft of a Freethinker 25

2   Kurt Vonnegut's Nonfiction Universe:
    "From all that crap, I have culled this volume" 33
    Considering and Reconsidering Nonfiction as a Genre 34
    Writing to Speak—The "Sweetly Faked Attention" of an Audience . .44
    "Making Jokes on Paper"—Writing Humor 49
    Considering and Reconsidering Reviews and Op-Ed Essays 54
    New Journalism—Writing in Search of Truth 59

3   *Slaughterhouse-Five*: Of Wars and America 65
    A Novel That Confronts the Novel 68
    Considering War—A Novel Unit 72
    Dissecting the United States of America 78
    The Big Questions of Life—Free Will, Time, and Human Dignity 79
    The Vonnegut Universe 82

    Traditional Concerns—The Canon and Kurt Vonnegut 84
    Expanding Critical Lenses for Students 86

4 *Cat's Cradle*: The Religion of Disbelief 89
    Of Religion, Science, and Art 91
    The Importance of Names and Words 95
    Parents, Children, and the Family 97
    Bokononism—Of Truth and Falsehood, and the Function
       of Myth 100
    Cat's Cradle as Symbolic Motif 103
    Cat's Cradle, the Book of Jonah, and *Moby-Dick* 104

5 *Player Piano* and *Galapagos*: The Evolution of
   Science and Technology 107
    Louise Rosenblatt and the Teaching of Literature—
       Teacher Assumptions and Biases within the
       Humanities and Sciences 108
    Dystopian Novel Unit—Sci-Fi Novels, and Movies 111
    Player Piano—Satire and Sci-Fi 115
    Player Piano—The Myth of Proteus 117
    Player Piano—America's View of Artists and Women 119
    Player Piano—Symbolism in an American Novel 121
    Galapagos—Evolution and the Teaching of Evolution 123
    Galapagos—Vonnegut as Part of the American Literary Tradition . . .125
    Galapagos—Science Fiction and Myth 127

6 *Bluebeard* and *Breakfast of Champions*: Art, Pop Art,
   and American Culture 131
    What Is Art?—The Role of Artists in the USA 132
    Vonnegut's Female Characters—Feminism and the
       Vonnegut Canon 136
    Stories and Journeys—Empowerment and a Homeric Motif 138
    Of Novels and Anti-Novels 141
    Warning: This Novel Is Explicit 143

7 *Welcome to the Monkey House*: Short Stories 149
    Examining and Evaluating the Short Story 150
    Becoming a Short Story Writer with Vonnegut 157
    Vonnegut's Stories—Artificial Intelligence, Ironic Science,
       and Free Will 162

Conclusion: Reading, Learning, Teaching Kurt Vonnegut 167

References 169

Acknowledgments

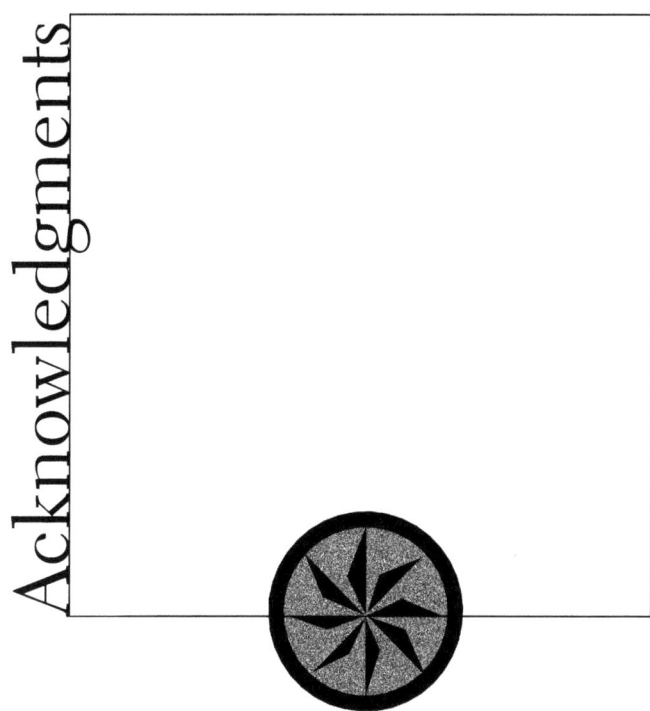

Writing multiple volumes of a series and editing an entire series are both dreams of mine as a writer and teacher, and they are the most daunting tasks I have ever attempted. As I mentioned in my first book in this series on Barbara Kingsolver, this volume could not have been possible without many, many people.

An odd coincidence occurred during the drafting of this book on Vonnegut. The author himself published once again and began appearing on TV and in print across the US, creating varying degrees of admiration and anger among those who have loved Vonnegut's work and those who revile his politics. The re-appraisal of Vonnegut that has occurred paralleled my own efforts to look even more closely at all of Vonnegut's work as a dedicated fan and a teacher.

In the spirit of community embraced by Vonnegut, I wish to thank the following for their contributions to the completion of this book:

- Yvonne Mason and her students at Hughes Academy (Greenville, SC) for reading and responding to Vonnegut's "Harrison Bergeron."
- The support and input of my editor for this book and series, Phyllis Korper.
- The support and inspiration provided by Joe Kincheloe.
- The students of Eng 11 J during the spring of 2006 at Furman University—a course dedicated to reading and writing with Kurt Vonnegut.
- The faculty and staff of the Education Department and the university at Furman.

- Family (Fran and Jessi, parents, and all), friends, colleagues, and students who are too numerous to name but invaluable to a writer and teacher.
- Kurt Vonnegut.

Introduction
"So It Goes"

Several years ago my new Honda Accord was dented on the passenger door. This occurred about the time repair businesses began offering to come to you and repair the dents with suction cups and a series of devices that magically brought the car back to brand new. Amazing!

One extremely hot summer day I stood in my driveway talking with the repairman while we both sweated and chatted. I can't recall *how* now, but we soon found ourselves deeply into a conversation about the writings of Kurt Vonnegut—a writer I had consumed throughout college and early adulthood (I regularly re-read *Breakfast of Champions*) but had eventually let slip away as if he didn't really matter. This young repairman had been an English major, and he still radiated with a passion for Vonnegut that turned up the summer temperature a few more notches. He also (as we might have guessed) planned to be a writer.

I immediately began rounding up all my copies of Vonnegut novels scattered throughout my bookshelf at home and my bookshelves in my classroom at the high school where I taught. The paperbacks were yellowed, torn, and musty—some with copyright dates from the sixties and many stamped by the various used bookstores where I had originally gathered the collection of Vonnegut's catalog.

Then it happened again. But this time for good.

I set out to buy new copies of *all* of Vonnegut's published works; then I re-read ever word by Vonnegut. This recommitment as a reader and an admirer of Vonnegut also involved bringing his short stories to all my classes and his novels to my Advanced Placement Literature and Composition students. *Slaughterhouse-Five* was my safe entry into assigning Vonnegut. But this sheepish introduction of Vonnegut to the reading list of a small southern high school quickly blossomed into students choosing to read *Breakfast of Champions* and *Welcome to the Monkey House* with a zeal I had rarely seen in an English class.

That journey must now be more than a decade old, and it is culminating in this book—a work that hopes to be a gift to teachers and students everywhere who may have lost Vonnegut as I had and those who still have not ventured into his world.

Writers are important—especially for the young, the young people who find themselves in high school and English classes where we confront ideas in the form of text. Vonnegut (1974) offers *why* they matter in his *Wampeters, Foma & Granfalloons*:

> I am persuaded that we [writers] are tremendously influential, even though most national leaders, my own included, probably never heard of most of us. . . . Our influence is slow and subtle, and it is felt mainly by the young. They are hungry for myths which resonate with the mysteries for their times.
>
> We give them those myths. (p. 230)

• • •

Many years ago, I sat with my Advanced Placement English and Literature class discussing the selection of poetry they had read the night before. This particular day comes easily to mind because I began telling the class the most outlandish, most unsupportable interpretations of one poem that a reasonable person could fabricate.

The students obediently jotted down most of what I said in the margins of their textbooks. Not a single question. Not a single challenge.

The next day I confessed and asked why no one had said a word in protest. Possibly more troubling than their silence and compliance the day before was their inability even to explain their own intellectual passivity. This group was very bright and exceptionally literate, but they were also *good students*.

In American classrooms, good students are nothing if not compliant—very quiet and very eager to absorb in order to repeat the required answers when requested (Scheele, 2004). In my more cynical moods, I refer to seasoned students as "intellectual zombies," and I blame many of our traditional practices in schools for the condition—

"SO IT GOES"

not the nature of children, not the deterioration of culture. And therein lies the motivation for this book.

While many aspects of American education have remained virtually unchanged for over a century, teachers today do face a certain raised intensity concerning some of the more harmful practices—prescriptive lesson planning, teacher-centered instruction, high-stakes testing, national and state standards, and potentially catastrophic accountability measures. Because of federal mandates such as No Child Left Behind (NCLB), our schools are often hostile to the genuine pleasure, passion, and uncertainty that can and should accompany teaching and learning, particularly teaching and learning with literature. Above all else, our schools value compliance by both teachers and students. There are to be no confrontations among people—or among ideas.

Yet if literature (all art, in fact) is anything, it is *confrontational.* Kafka (1979), in a letter to Oskar Pollak, wrote that "[a] book must be the axe for the frozen sea inside us" (p. 290). For him, literature confronted the paralysis that life imposed on him. Interestingly, Ernst Pawell (1984) states simply about Kafka: "He hated school" (p. 26). For me, there is a profound connection here. Our traditional approaches to school—stressing standardization, silence, analysis, quantification (Thomas, 2004), and objectivity—work directly in opposition to the very nature of literature, the heart of English classrooms, confrontation. Kafka's metaphor of the sea fits well the belief I hold about the nature of Self and of teaching and learning; the sea is an ever-moving, ever-evolving thing that is defined by its movement and constant change. Once frozen, it loses its nature.

This book will offer an opportunity for teachers and students to *confront* "the frozen sea inside us," inside our schools, and inside our literature and writing curriculums through the varied writing of what they teach and how they teach as well (see the Introduction and Appendix of *Reading, Learning, Teaching Barbara Kingsolver,* 2005).

• • •

"I keep losing and regaining my equilibrium, which is the basic plot of all popular fiction. And I myself am a work of fiction"— Vonnegut (1974) acknowledges the mercurial nature of a writer's fictional and real worlds (*Wampeters, Foma & Granfaloons,* p. xix). With that in mind, Chapter One will explore the life of Vonnegut but will quickly move to a brief introduction to the many and varied works of the writer. I will detail the essential themes and concerns that run throughout his writing along with discussing the characteristics that make Vonnegut's writing distinct.

Chapter Two looks at the collections of Vonnegut's nonfiction as a means of considering nonfiction and genres in general; further, it offers opportunities for students to read and write nonfiction, speeches, and book reviews while exploring the blurred lines between techniques that characterize fiction and nonfiction. Vonnegut's most celebrated novel, *Slaughterhouse-Five,* is the focus of Chapter Three, where we will investigate how art addresses war. Religion as a topic of fiction stands as the center of Chapter Four on *Cat's Cradle.* Vonnegut's ubiquitous interest in science, technology, and evolution dominates two of his novels—*Galapagos* and *Player Piano;* Chapter Five focuses on these works and topics.

Vonnegut's own life as a visual artist is an aspect of his career few people recognize; Chapter Six centers on Vonnegut's major statement on art in *Bluebeard* and Vonnegut's own confrontation of America and pop culture through *Breakfast of Champions.* Some of the most accessible works by Vonnegut are his short stories. "Harrison Bergeron" and his other stories have found a home in school anthologies. Chapter Seven deals with his major collection of short fiction, *Welcome to the Monkey House,* and with the short story form in general.

Woven through the chapters will be several related approaches to Vonnegut—**Entry Points, Connections**, and **Student Insight**. Entry Points will offer brief works such as poems, songs, essays, and short stories that can serve to open a lesson or unit on a longer Vonnegut work. The Connections provide examples of related works (novels, essays, short stories, poems, movies) that can be taught in conjunction with Vonnegut, as part of a larger unit including Vonnegut, or as a follow-up unit to a Vonnegut unit. Student Insight sections include actual student work samples from lessons on Vonnegut from any classrooms.

Chapter One

Kurt Vonnegut

You Can Take the Man out of the War, But You Can't Take the War out of the Man—Writer as Freethinker and Passivist

"I keep losing and regaining my equilibrium, which is the basic plot of all popular fiction. And I myself am a work of fiction," Vonnegut (1974) explains in the preface to his *Wampeters, Foma & Granfalloons* (p. xix). As is the case with most writers, distilling the biography from the fiction is a challenge with Vonnegut. We can argue that much of his life runs throughout his fiction just as we can clearly see the details of his life revealed throughout his books of nonfiction. While knowing fully the life of Vonnegut is not easy or even possible, it is valuable for readers, students, and teachers to explore what his life *might* be. So in the beginning of this chapter we will explore the life of Kurt Vonnegut, who has lived a most remarkable life as he simultaneously wrote into being alternate worlds out of the fabric of his life.

From the stuff of his living we will move to the stuff of his thinking—the thematic concerns that dominate his work. These themes recur in his fiction and his nonfiction; they resonate when he has given speeches and when he has offered his voice to the greater struggles of all humanity. While none of these thematic concerns prove to be novel, clearly Vonnegut's wrestling with them strikes his readers in ways that they would have never predicted.

We will end this chapter by looking at the craft of Vonnegut as a writer—the craft that renders his ideas unique and vital for us as readers, students, or teachers. This chapter will serve as a foundation for coming to know Vonnegut the man and the writer. I hope that foundation serves the readers of this book well so that they can find themselves buried as deeply and lovingly in Vonnegut's world as I am.

Also in the preface to *Wampeters,* Vonnegut (1974) muses, "Only when we have overcome loneliness can we begin to share wealth and work more fairly" (p. xxii). I believe Vonnegut may trust that his writing can lead us down that path to the "artificial families of a thousand members or more" he argues will save us all (p. xxii). It dawns on me that many of our schools are ready and able to serve as such families, and I am convinced Vonnegut's words can serve us well within our varied classrooms.

Vonnegut as Fact and Fiction— The Life of a Writer

Having spent several years of doctoral work as a biographer, I fully appreciate the value of knowing the life of someone as remarkable and prolific as Vonnegut. I also recognize the limitations of dealing with that life story briefly in a work such as this. Since we can access chronologies of Vonnegut's life quite easily and fully via the Internet (see The Vonnegut Web www.vonnegutweb.com—and click on "Chronology") and since most critical works include some biographical sketches (Allen, 1991; Schatt, 1976; Marvin, 2002; Boon, 2001), I will discuss here the key elements of Vonnegut's life that seem to fall into fairly clear categories or themes that run through his writings— his schooling, his military experiences, his work, and his family life.

Born in Indianapolis on November 11, 1922, Vonnegut was raised in both a profoundly unusual home (a home devoted to freethinking) and an inescapably traumatic home (one that included suicide). He is the son of Kurt and Edith Vonnegut; he grew up with a brother, Bernard, and a sister, Alice—the brother born in 1914 and the sister, in 1917. Vonnegut himself often notes the strong impact being raised in a family of freethinkers had on him, his works punctuated with references to his relatives, exposure to socialists through his uncle Alex (Marvin, 2002)—detailed, for example, in the opening to *Jailbird*—and Eugene Debs, a socialist whose stock was certainly quite different in more conservative families across the U.S. during Vonnegut's childhood.

In an odd way, formal schooling created several key influences on Vonnegut although he never achieved the type of academic success we might imagine for a literary person. Shortridge High School provided Vonnegut with an experience that few young writers had available to them in the 1930s: "Writing for a daily newspaper made Vonnegut aware of his audience at an age when most people are writing only for their teachers" (Marvin, 2002, p. 4). Vonnegut continued his interest in journalism at Cornell University by writing for the student newspaper; his first college experience also revealed his budding interest in science when he became a biochemistry major—although he eventually chose the arts over the sciences in his professional life. After his military career during World War II, Vonnegut returned to college at the University of Chicago, pursuing a graduate degree in anthropology. His shift in scientific interests later revealed itself more fully in his fiction, but his final attempt to achieve traditional academic success is more revealing since his master's thesis was rejected—leaving him without a degree (although the university bestowed the degree on him in 1971 after he became a well-known writer).

Possibly the key period of Vonnegut's life was those years in the military that disrupted Vonnegut's college experience. Vonnegut enlisted in the U.S. army in 1943. The irony of his German ancestry punctuates the most well-known aspects of his biography: The Germans took Vonnegut as a prisoner of war at the Battle of the Bulge (Marvin, 2002). This event would stand as the most dramatic event in most anyone's life, but Vonnegut's equally doomed and charmed life took yet another twist when as a POW he found himself in a subterranean meat locker in Dresden during the Allied firebombing of that city. Vonnegut survived WWII, life as a POW, and the firebombing on February 13, 1945—"the largest massacre in European history" (Marvin, 2002, p. 6). In May of 1945, after his safe return, Vonnegut received the Purple Heart and was released from the military, although his life as a soldier would never leave him and in many ways would haunt him until the publication of his WWII novel, *Slaughterhouse-Five*, in the late 1960s.

As noted earlier, Vonnegut's release from the military led to his last attempt at the academic life; it also set the stage for his journey as a *professional*. The lure of journalism pulled Vonnegut into being a reporter for the Chicago City News Bureau while he attended the University of Chicago. His diploma-less departure from the university in 1947 seems to have contributed to his essentially stumbling into his first major job as an adult. Vonnegut's brother Bernard, a well-respected scientist at General Electric in Schenectady, New York, secured Kurt a job in public relations there. The writing career that would emerge had its genesis in his first attempts at short fiction, written at night during his first years at GE. "'Report on the Barnhouse Effect" was sold to *Collier's* for as much money as Vonnegut earned at GE in a month and a half, $750 (Marvin, 2002). The first half of the twentieth century proved to be fertile ground for short fiction writers in America, from F. Scott Fitzgerald to J. D. Salinger; this avenue to creative expression and financial security soon lured Vonnegut to quit his day job at GE in 1951.

Here marked the moment when Vonnegut the writer came into existence *in fact,* but the genesis would not be as easy or seamless as we tend to explain in hindsight. Vonnegut worked as a teacher and an advertising agent; he even opened a Saab dealership over the next several years. Though he began writing and publishing short fiction and even his first novel, in 1952, Vonnegut would not find his feet on firm ground for many years. From the early 1950s until today, we can call Vonnegut a professional writer, but he has also taught in writing programs on a number of occasions—the University of Iowa in the 1960s and Harvard in the 1970s, for example. A 1967 Guggenheim Fellowship and the publication of *Slaughterhouse-Five* in 1969 probably stand as the major turning points for Vonnegut as a successful writer. We will discuss throughout this book the shifting respect Vonnegut has received from critics and fans, but I feel safe in arguing that since the late 1960s, Vonnegut has secured a spot as a major American writer.

"A *granfalloon* is a proud and meaningless association of human beings," Vonnegut (1974) explains in the Preface to *Wampeters, Foma & Granfalloons,* a collection of nonfiction that includes his "Biafra: A People Betrayed." This essay on Africa and much of Vonnegut's writings eventually drift to his deep concern for family, both literal and created. Vonnegut's own families have proven to be crucial details of his life and essential elements of his writing. I have noted above his German ancestry and touched on briefly his home life as a child. In 1944, during his military service, Vonnegut's mother committed suicide, a traumatic event that reveals itself in many ways in his works. After his Dresden experience, Vonnegut returned to the U.S. and married Jane Marie Cox in 1945; two years later, they had a son, Mark, and then daughters Edith and Nanette in the 1950s. Vonnegut's father died in 1957, and this was followed soon by the death of his sister Alice, who succumbed to cancer just days after her husband was killed in a train wreck. This series of overwhelming losses resulted in an immense shift in Vonnegut's life—he and his wife adopted three of his nephews.

Kurt and Jane Vonnegut found themselves raising six children in the 1960s, well before Vonnegut had secured financial success as a writer. The extended nature of this new family parallels Vonnegut's own call for extended families in his works. Yet, his marriage failed by 1971, when he and Jane separated. More problems followed when his son Mark suffered an emotional collapse in 1972. Vonnegut himself began to deal with his own emotional and psychological troubles in the 1970s, taking Ritalin for a while before seeking sessions with a psychologist. Since the publication of *Slaughterhouse-Five,* Vonnegut has experienced a fluctuating reputation and fan base, but he has remained a prominent writer and speaker over the past thirty-plus years. In 1979, he married Jill Krementz, a photojournalist. Vonnegut has produced a substantial list of works; he also continues to find himself in the role of survivor after a house fire in 2000 left him with pneumonia. *Timequake* (1997) was his last novel as of this writing, but he published *Bagombo Snuff Box: Uncollected Short Fiction* and *God Bless You, Dr. Kevorkian* in 1999; then in 2005 he published *A Man without a Country,* collection of essays. Marvin (2002) has recently noted a work-in-progress for Vonnegut as well, titled *If God Were Alive Today* (p. 12).

The Works of Vonnegut

Vonnegut's reputation as a respected novelist and writer certainly depends heavily on the pivotal positive reception of his best-known work, *Slaughterhouse-Five* (1969). By the mid-1970s critical response to his writing was in its earliest phase, but the essential debate on his importance and value as an American writer had already begun: "Kurt Vonnegut, Jr., has been labeled at various times as a mediocre science-fiction writer, a social satirist, a Black Humorist, and a major novelist" (Schatt, 1976, p. 1).

While this volume certainly argues that Vonnegut is a valuable writer for our society, for all of humanity, and for students everywhere, I also recognize that the artistic *quality* Vonnegut's work achieves is debatable within the literary world. I will stand on Vonnegut's own assessment of his career, offered in 1998:

> When I look back at my incredibly lucky career as a writer, it seems that there was never time to think. It was as though I were skiing down a steep and hazardous mountain slope. When I look back at the marks my skis made in the snow on the way down, I only now realize that I wrote again and again about people who behaved decently in an indecent society. (Boon, 2001, viii)

The body of Vonnegut's work includes over twenty book-length publications, primarily consisting of novels. He has also offered four works of nonfiction (Vonnegut surprised many by publishing *A Man without a Country* in 2005), one play, a couple of collections of short fiction, and *God Bless You, Dr. Kevorkian* (1999), which fittingly seems to defy classification. The following chapters will deal with six of his novels at length, addressing his nonfiction and short fiction in separate chapters. Here, I will briefly introduce all of his works as an introduction to the impressive catalog offered by Vonnegut since the mid-1900s.

Player Piano (1952) introduced the reading world to Vonnegut in a fitting manner; it is often called a science fiction novel (re-issued by the publisher in 1954 with a more aggressively science fiction title (*Utopia 14*), a dystopian novel and a post-World War II satire (Marvin, 2002). Interestingly, critics and fans alike have discounted all of these labels with equal fervor. That this novel is difficult to classify and difficult to summarize is evidence of the complexity of the work that makes it suitable for the classroom. The novel follows the disintegrating life of Paul Proteus in the futuristic world after a third world war. In this particular future, Vonnegut draws a world completely mechanized, a world driven by quantifications of intelligence and of each human's station in life. Much of this novel seems to be culled from Vonnegut's own experiences at GE, and it clearly establishes his concern for the tension between mechanistic science and humanity. We will examine this novel in depth in Chapter Five along with *Galapagos*—both highly science-oriented works.

Although I will not deal with *The Sirens of Titan* (1959) at length in this book, critics and readers hold Vonnegut's second novel in high esteem. Marvin (2002) notes that it "is the easiest [novel] to classify as science fiction" and argues that the novel actually "employs the conventions of science fiction, not for their own sake, but for the power they give him to explore the meaning and value of human life in a technological age" (p. 43). The plot revolves around Malachi Constant of Hollywood, the richest American man in the twenty-second century. Winston Niles Rumfoord, a secondary character, also has great wealth. Both characters experience space and time travel—events that will appear in similar detail in *Slaughterhouse-Five*. This novel introduces the term "chrono-synclastic infundibulum," referring to the coexistence of time and concepts throughout the universe (though this is a drastic oversimplification of the concept here and in other novels by Vonnegut). The work directly explores Vonnegut's interests in science, but it also addresses religion and most of the key themes that recur throughout Vonnegut's novels (we will explore those themes further in the next section).

Schatt (1976) describes *Mother Night* (1961) as "a marked change . . . in terms of both subject matter and narrative technique" since it deals with World War II and presents itself as a memoir by the main character, Howard W. Campbell, Jr., an American playwright living in Germany and functioning as a secret agent (p. 43). This confessional novel allows Vonnegut to move beyond the science fiction label and pursue his critique of the horrors of war. Through Campbell, Vonnegut shows the moral and political struggles of the character while also laying out those struggles in universal ways. Here, too, Vonnegut presents readers and students with the unreliable first-person narrator, in the tradition of Mark Twain's Huck Finn.

CONNECTION

Mother Night shares some interesting parallels with the movie *Confessions of a Dangerous Mind* (2003) based on the controversial memoir (*Confessions of a Dangerous Mind: An Unauthorized Autobiography,* 1982/2002) by TV celebrity Chuck Barris, who reached a certain level of fame in the 1970s with game shows such as "The Dating Game," "The Gong Show," and "The Newlywed Game." In Vonnegut's novel and the Barris-based movie and memoir, we see both the creative and spy worlds interact. All three of these works also ask that the audience swim through intricate layers of the tragic and the comic, leaving the reader or viewer often torn over how to respond. Since Barris's memoir offers a premise that many people find outlandish—that he was a CIA assassin during the Cold War—students may want to dispute the veracity of Barris's claims, particularly if they are faced with the possibility that Barris lifted his story from Vonnegut—a provocative claim that can be neither proven nor refuted, much like Barris's assertions. (Note that *Mother Night* was made into a movie in 1996, directed by Keith Gordon and starring Nick Nolte and Alan Arkin.)

CONNECTION

Schatt (1976) explains that in *Mother Night* "[t]he point of view is very similar to that found in Vladimir Nabokov's *Lolita* since both Humbert Humbert and Campbell are imprisoned monsters by society's standards" (p. 43). An effective study of unreliable narrators could include *Mother Night, The Adventures of Huckleberry Finn,* and *Lolita*. Classes could be divided into three groups, one for each novel, and asked to focus on the morality of the narrators (both as perceived by the readers and by the societies within which each narrator exists). The relative nature of perspectives and morality (Is morality bound by the assumptions of the society?) can be explored through all three novels. Students will find many similarities but enough nuances to make such discussions rich.

Cat's Cradle (1963) captures in many ways the abilities and deepest concerns of Vonnegut as both philosopher and writer. The novel is a complex satire of religion, a warning about the apocalyptic potential of science, and a contemplation in action about the novel form and writing. The characters include the narrator John and the family of John Hoenikker, the father of the atom bomb and the inventor of ice-nine (which causes the end of the world). The novel introduces the readers to the Bokononian religion and some of the terminology that keeps resurfacing in Vonnegut's work—"wampeter," "foma," and "granfalloon" (all resurrected in *Wampeters, Foma & Grandfalloons*). Chapter Four will devote an expanded discussion primarily to issues of religion raised by Vonnegut in this novel.

God Bless You, Mr. Rosewater (1965) offers an unforgettable title, a refrain of sorts from the world of Vonnegut that is echoed in *God Bless You, Dr. Kevorkian* (1999). While we often associate Vonnegut with debates concerning science and religion, his work typically addresses issues of wealth and poverty as well. This novel centers on Eliot Rosewater, who creates the Rosewater Foundation in Rosewater, Indiana, as a response to his own growing moral sense that contrasts his great wealth. The plot is less dynamic than the questions raised by Vonnegut concerning wealth and poverty, degrees of sanity (or insanity), tensions between liberal and conservative politics, and the relative nature of social expectations on individuals.

ENTRY POINT

In *God Bless You, Mr. Rosewater,* Marvin (2002) explains, "Senator Rosewater uses the techniques that Orwell criticizes" in "Politics and the English Language" (1946/1968) "to convince his constituents that the rich deserve everything they have, and sharing anything with the poor will only make them lazy" (p. 19). Since Vonnegut notes Orwell as a source, Orwell's essay on political language serves well as an entry point into Vonnegut's novel. Orwell's discussion of the manipulation of language for political gain is a valuable discussion for English students—or any students—and provides a foundation for exploring one of Vonnegut's most memorable characters, Rosewater, and for unpacking some of Vonnegut's recurring themes concerning politics, wealth, and poverty.

Welcome to the Monkey House (1968) has stood as Vonnegut's official collection of some of his short fiction, a form that provided him with early financial gain. This collection of short stories will be discussed in depth in Chapter Seven, but I will note here that his stories are quite accessible for students, and they offer glimpses into the tendencies of Vonnegut that are more fully formed in his novels. "Harrison Bergeron" is the most anthologized story by Vonnegut, as well known as his *Slaughterhouse-Five;* the story has wonderfully crafted humor and biting satire—dealing with the perennial concern in the American psyche for the dangers of oppressive governments often associated with communism and socialism. While the content is highly complex and sophisticated, the story shows that Vonnegut can expose difficult content matter in dynamic and comic ways that allow even less mature readers to deal with the subtleties of human free will within social constraints.

Chapter Three focuses on Vonnegut's pivotal work, *Slaughterhouse-Five* (1969), and the complex nature of war novels. Vonnegut admits that it took him over twenty years to address his own experience as a prisoner of war during the firebombing of Dresden, a horrific moment in World War II that is often ignored by Americans. The novel stands as a dramatic and experimental consideration of war; it also fits perfectly within the disillusionment growing in America during the Vietnam conflict that seemed to weigh on every aspect of life in the U.S. in the 1960s. This novel is Vonnegut's most read and most celebrated. It follows the life of Billy Pilgrim, like Vonnegut, a POW during the firebombing of Dresden. This novel takes the reader on a journey that manipulates and considers time in nonlinear ways; Vonnegut also asks the reader to reconsider many assumptions about the novel form and about narration. The highly sophisticated nature of Vonnegut's form and topic make this novel ideal for our classrooms.

Vonnegut's only play, *Happy Birthday, Wanda June* (1971), modernizes the story of Ulysses and Penelope in order to satirize macho behavior embodied in the American novelist Ernest Hemingway. The characters are Harold Ryan (modeled on Hemingway) and his wife Penelope, who carries on with her life, along with her son Paul, after Harold disappears on an expedition in the Amazon. Eight years after the disappearance, however, Harold returns to the family to find everything changed.

CONNECTIONS

Lawrence R. Broer (Boon, 2001, p. 66) notes that "Vonnegut views Hemingway as an artist of the highest order" and that Vonnegut's works often involve Hemingway in some way—*Happy Birthday, Wanda June; Palm Sunday; Deadeye Dick; Bluebeard;* and *Fates Worse than Death*. The stories and novels of Hemingway make excellent companion works to Vonnegut's catalogue. Both writers have qualities that make them uniquely American, particularly their connections with journalism, and both writers grew out of the two great wars of the twentieth century. As well, each writer offers many themes, techniques, and styles that are *unlike* the other.

As a dedicated fan of *Breakfast of Champions* (1973), I have always felt somewhat disappointed by critics' displeasure with the novel, but

Vonnegut's own grading of the novel as a "C" truly hits where it hurts (*Palm Sunday,* p. 284). As an experiment in the novel and as a satire of American pop culture, however, I will look at the uses of this novel in Chapter Six. The story revolves heavily around the recurring icon of Vonnegut's work, Kilgore Trout, and the richly drawn Hoover family, a mixture of oddities that defies any sort of synopsis. This novel also offers the classroom an opportunity to consider both the novel and movie drawn from the novel since *Breakfast of Champions* did find its way to the screen with notable actors Bruce Willis and Nick Nolte. The work deals with science fiction by following Trout in a much more expanded role than in other works, and it proves to be as much a philosophical consideration and a literary exploration as anything else.

Wampeters, Foma & Granfalloons (1974) is the first of four book-length works of nonfiction by Vonnegut (all of which are discussed in Chapter Two). Subtitled "Opinions," this collection draws its title from those three terms in *Cat's Cradle.* Here, Vonnegut collects many of his notable speeches and includes what he admits are samples of New Journalism—"Am I a New Journalist? I guess" (p. xvii). Vonnegut's piece on the people of Biafra, which highlights his concern for the extended family and for the oppression of disempowered people, and his interview for *Playboy* are notable selections in the collection.

Slapstick (1976) opens with the sentence "This is the closest I will ever come to writing an autobiography" (p. 1). Vonnegut explains that the title grew from his own affection for classic comedians Laurel and Hardy. Dr. Wilbur Daffodil-11 Swain is the last U.S. president, who has a number of freakish physical characteristics and a relationship with an equally unusual twin sister that challenges any reader's ability to suspend normal expectations for novels and relationships among characters. Schatt (1976) explains that much of the novel grew from Vonnegut's own experiences with the deaths of his uncle Alex and his sister Alice (from cancer), whose own tragic death came only two days after her husband was killed in a train accident (pp. 110–111). Here, the plot and characterizations seem the stuff of science fiction, but the work primarily explores human loneliness and the benefits of deep and extended family relationships. Although the novel is quite dark, it is also truly a comic novel.

"Yes—Kilgore Trout is back again," greets readers of *Jailbird* (1979, p. 1). This political satire is framed by Vonnegut in his "Prologue" as a memoir of Vonnegut's luncheon arranged by his conservative uncle, Alex, that included his father and Powers Hapgood. The opening also sketches a labor clash and massacre for the reader and establishes Vonnegut's passion for the powerless and often oppressed workers in the larger American capitalist system. The novel's main character, "Walter F. Starbuck, . . . was accidentally shaped by the Massacre, even though it took place on Christmas morning in eighteen hundred ninety-four, long before Starbuck was born" (*Jailbird,* p. 15). While the novel pulls many aspects of U.S. history together in a narrative form, Vonnegut here offers a satirical look at the Watergate scandal, at the essentially corrupt nature of political and bureaucratic life, as portrayed by the imprisoned Starbuck.

ENTRY POINT

In a brief passage of his progressive history of the U.S., Zinn (1995) acknowledges the unjust execution of Nicola Sacco and Bartolomeo Vanzetti (p. 367), the subject of Vonnegut's reminiscence concerning a lunch conversation among him, his father, and Powers Hapgood (*Jailbird,* p. 14). This novel also quotes Sacco's letter to his thirteen-year-old son before his execution, the same letter quoted by Zinn. The Sacco and Vanzetti incident is one of many moments in U.S. history that has fallen through the cracks. Serving as a focal point for Vonnegut's concern for social justice, this unjust execution also is the focus of Barbara Kingsolver's poem, "For Sacco and Vanzetti" (*Another America,* 1998), which can serve as a vivid entry point into this moment in history that students need to begin to place Vonnegut's commentary within *Jailbird* into both the larger context of U.S. history and their own lives.

In *Palm Sunday* (1981), Vonnegut presents his readers with what he subtitles as *An Autobiographical Collage;* the collection consists of letters, essays, speeches, interviews, reviews, commencement addresses, a short story, and even a sermon by Vonnegut—showing that Vonnegut takes the term "collage" quite seriously. This collection will be included in Chapter Two, notably as we ask students to write speeches. This collection is characterized as a hybrid work of fiction and nonfiction by Vonnegut—"This book combines the tidal power of a major novel with the bone-rattling immediacy of front-line journalism" (p. xi). Therefore, it suits discussions of genre and form, particularly for students still developing sophisticated understandings of these somewhat artificial labels.

Deadeye Dick (1982) is a fictional memoir by Rudy Waltz, who carries the nickname "Deadeye Dick." "Midland City has now been depopulated by a neutron bomb explosion. It was a big news story for about ten days or so," captures the tragic-comic nature of Vonnegut's subject matter as it collides with his narrator's attiude (p. 35). This novel has many of the elements we associate with Vonnegut—a concern for the dangers of technology and preparing for war, the single perspective of a richly drawn and unique narrator/main character, and the human pursuit of certainty and understanding in the face of chaos. The ultimate inability of humanity to address these problems is captured ominously in the novel's final lines: "You want to know something? We are still in the Dark Ages. The Dark Ages—they haven't ended yet" (p. 271).

As noted earlier, *Galapagos* (1985) is discussed in Chapter Five along with *Player Piano* as we consider Vonnegut's opinion of technology and science. *Galapagos* is a wonderfully realized novel in that Vonnegut breathes life into evolutionary theory through fiction. Jeff Karon (Boon, 2001) notes Vonnegut's ironic use of a "disembodied narrator" that "pushes us to probe questions of meaning and metaphysics" (p. 115). Time, science, narration, and many elements of Vonnegut's writing are manipulated here as he forces the reader to think deeply about what we still debate—the origin of humans and whether Charles Darwin has us on the right path. The narrator of this novel reminds us that "[o]ne million years ago, back in 1986 A.D., . . . [h]umans beings had much bigger brains back then than they do today" (p. 3).

Readers of Vonnegut are often immediately drawn to the stark artwork that appears in his novels—notably the larger role played by the childlike drawings of shockingly adult subject matter in *Breakfast of Champions,* the genesis of Rabo Karabekian. *Bluebeard* (1987) stands as a tour-de-force commentary on the art world and the nature of art. This novel and these elements are the topic of Chapter Six. In his "Author's Note," Vonnegut warns that his novel is "a hoax autobiography," but "[i]t is not to be taken as a responsible history of the Abstract Expressionist school of painting." Through the eyes of narrator Rabo Karabekian, however, we are shepherded through the art world, both as a way for Vonnegut to ask us to reconsider the nature of art and as a way to criticize that art world for allowing monetary wealth to dictate who and what matters in that art world.

"Just because some of us can read and write and do a little math, that doesn't mean we deserve to conquer the Universe," ends *Hocus Pocus* (1990), a novel fabricated from thousands of slips of paper used by Eugene Debs Hartke, the fictional author and main character of the novel. Fittingly, Vonnegut dedicates the novel to Eugene V. Debs, who "had become a Socialist while in jail in the Pullman strike" (Zinn, 1995, p. 332) and stands as the personification of Vonnegut's concern for the plight of oppressed people. The novel also allows Vonnegut to ruminate on the Vietnam War, as Hartke is a veteran of that war. Hartke taunts those who expected the Apocalypse at the turn of the millennium (the novel is set in 2001)—though the end of the world remains at the center of this work.

CONNECTION

Donald E. Morse (Boon, 2001) notes that "[u]nlike in Arthur C. Clarke and Stanley Kubrick's *2001*, in Vonnegut's millennial novel, *Hocus Pocus*, humans will not travel to other parts of the universe in the new century, nor will they receive help from some mysterious source outside themselves, this planet, or this solar system" (p. 97). With the false threat of Y2K coinciding with most of the world mistakenly anticipating the new millennium one year too early in 2000 and with our students having lived through the actual turning of the millennium in 2001, pairing *Hocus Pocus* with Clarke's novel or Kurbick's movie is a fertile opportunity for students to consider the human obsession with arbitrary changes in our calendar and with the many predictions of the end of time throughout human history. Many futuristic and Apocalyptic works of art present a surface that seems to be concerned with the future, while the ultimate message is a direct commentary on *now* or on the essential qualities of human nature and civilization.

Subtitled *An Autobiographical Collage, Fates Worse Than Death* (1991) serves as "a sequel," according to Vonnegut, to the book sharing that subtitle (*Palm Sunday*). I will return to this and the other nonfiction books by Vonnegut in Chapter Two. As a collection of speeches and Vonnegut's commentaries on his own life, this volume serves a similar purpose to *Palm Sunday,* simply adding a decade of living in between. If we are uncertain that nonfiction can achieve a level of timelessness found in fiction, we have to look no further than this collection, when Vonnegut complains: "I listen to the ethical pronouncements of the leaders of the so-called religious revival going on in this country, including those of our President," and he concludes that Americans are being urged to "'Stop thinking'" and "'Obey'" (p. 158). Was this written in the 1980s—or 2006?

Timequake (1997) was, according to Vonnegut himself, the last novel for this author. "I had the timequake zap everybody and everything in an instant from February 13th, 2001, back to February 17th, 1991. Then we all had to get back to 2001 the hard way," captures the essential plot of this novel, which takes Vonnegut's manipulation of time to an even higher level than in his other works (p. xiii). In a simplistic way, we might say this is Vonnegut's commentary on humanity, the U.S., and the world at the arbitrary turn of the millennium.

"No matter how clumsily I wrote when I started out, there were magazines that would publish such orangutans," notes Vonnegut in his "Coda to My Career as a Writer for Periodicals" in *Bagombo Snuff Box: Uncollected Short Fiction* (1999, p. 289). Vonnegut has collected the stories he had previously allowed to lie dormant in the many magazines where he began his career as a writer of popular short fiction. English teachers searching for works by Vonnegut that most students could not have possibly seen might want to look through this collection that offers many works that would fit well in the classroom, although I will not deal with any in the following chapters.

God Bless You, Dr. Kevorkian (1999) echoes the title of one of Vonnegut's most loved works, *God Bless You, Mr. Rosewater*. This razor thin collection announces itself as a series of interviews conducted in the afterlife with the assistance of Dr. Jack Kevorkian and broadcast on radio station WNYC. The introduction emphasizes Vonnegut's humanist roots: "I am a humanist, which means, in part that I have tried to behave decently without any expectation of rewards or punishments after I'm dead" (p. 9). Vonnegut's afterlife interviews include Clarence Darrow, Eugene Victor Debs, Adolf Hitler, James Earl Ray, Shakespeare, Kilgore Trout, and Isaac Asimov, to name a few. This tiny book can serve as a wonderful source of opening read-aloud passages for any English class or as a text for a brief lesson since the sections are quite short but also exhibit the many gifts of Vonnegut.

CONNECTION

"My German-American ancestors . . . called themselves 'Freethinkers,'" explains Vonnegut in *God Bless You, Dr. Kevorkian* (1999, p. 9). As "humanist," "agnostic," "atheist," and "Freethinker" are keys terms and concepts to understanding Vonnegut's philosophical core, students can benefit from reading Susan Jacoby's insightful and revealing *Freethinkers: A History of American Secularism* (2004). This study by Jacoby explores many of the major names in U.S. history and argues that much of American ideology has humanism and freethinking at its roots—although the popular perception is that American society is almost exclusively based on Judeo-Christian ethics (and historically composed of orthodox Christians). Jacoby gives many of the people who populate Vonnegut's references a new life as she weaves the story of America and its primary thinkers throughout the past two hundred plus years.

Vonnegut published nonfiction pieces in the alternative magazine *In These Times* after the turn of the millennium; he broke his vow of publishing no more with the publication of *A Man without a Country* (2005), adding a fourth full-length collection of nonfiction to his catalog. The book is punctuated with Vonnegut artwork—a series of handwritten mini-posters with Vonnegut aphorisms, a few Vonnegut drawings, and the occasional Vonnegut asterisk. In the opening piece,

KURT VONNEGUT 19

Vonnegut shares a story of his childhood and his early epiphany about humor: "And then I found out that a joke was a way to break into an adult conversation" (p. 2). This collection may fairly be called the culmination of that realization since humor is the technique Vonnegut uses to break into adult conversations in the early years of the twenty-first century—commenting on America, politicians, and virtually every topic he has scoured throughout his career. This surprise publication also resurrected the public Vonnegut as he began to make TV appearances near the publication of the book in September of 2005.

Thoughts of a Freethinker— Themes and Concerns in Vonnegut's Work

Boon (2001) explains that Vonnegut continues "a trend in American literature that began with Benjamin Franklin[;] Vonnegut's style is ripe with irony and full of aphoristic wit" (p. x). For students and teachers, we need to acknowledge and unpack the themes and concerns Vonnegut wraps inside the irony and the wit. Like many writers with extensive catalogs of published works, Vonnegut can be accused of returning often to favorite arguments and anchoring themes, but as we will discuss throughout this book, Vonnegut's revisiting of those themes moves beyond his being a one-trick pony and offers readers nuanced and complex explorations of those concepts as he shifts his stance on those recurring themes. While we may characterize him as concerned with science, the Vonnegut of *Player Piano* is not the Vonnegut of *Galapagos,* or the Vonnegut of *Timequake.*

The family and the extended family

In Vonnegut's own life, he found himself adopting three of his sister's children after her death from cancer, creating his own complex and unusual family. Throughout many of his works, Vonnegut argues for the need to form extended and artificial families. Marvin (2002) notes that "Vonnegut also criticizes the capitalist system for encouraging people to think of themselves as individuals rather than as members of extended families" (p. 20). Vonnegut names two types of such families in *Cat's Cradle* (and uses one of the terms in his first collection of nonfiction)—a "karass" ("a team organized by God to do His will") and a "granfalloon" ("a meaningless association of people, such as a fraternal group or a nation")—but includes examples of the need for families throughout many of his works (Marvin, 2002, p. 20). In essence, he argues for the best kind of socialism in contrast to the demonized perception of socialism and communism in the popular American psyche. "Humanists, having received no credible information about any sort of God, are content to serve as well as they can, the only abstraction with which they have some familiarity: their communities," Vonnegut (1999b) has stated recently in *God Bless You, Dr. Kevorkian*—blending his socialistic and agnostic tendencies to form what we might call a sense of social justice Vonnegut himself would ascribe to the teachings of Jesus.

Technology, science, and humanity

From his first full-length book, *Player Piano,* Vonnegut has persisted in asking humans to develop a much more skeptical eye than we have for technological advances, for the promises offered by science. The odd thing about Vonnegut is that he "admires the curiosity and ingenuity of scientists"—notably that of his own brother—but he also "condemns their failure to look up from their microscopes and consider the consequences of their discoveries" (Marvin, 2002, p. 21). His characters both suffer the worst-case scenarios of technology and science gone terribly wrong and speak as skeptical and moral harbingers of those disasters. Morse (Boon, 2001) offers that Vonnegut sees the dangers of technology intertwined with war and rampant capitalism—"The neutron bomb [in *Deadeye Dick*] becomes an apt symbol for this kind of progress measured by corporate bottom lines" (p. 96). As anyone who reads and studies many of Vonnegut's books comes to see, Vonnegut doesn't so much fear technology or science as he fears technology/science, war, and capitalism when all three forces converge with no moral barometer to guide the way.

Organizations versus individual humans

Vonnegut's belief in the best socialism has to offer and his criticism of American rugged individualism do not lessen his deep concern for individual humans—and the dignity that all humanity deserves. For students, this subtle distinction is quite challenging, but Vonnegut, like American educator and philosopher John Dewey, believes all societies and all individuals are always equally sacred. In the idealized world of Vonnegut, a society formed to benefit the humanity of all of its members is quite distinct from the traditional organizations that dominate modern American life—churches, business, schools, governments. While humans should be constantly searching to form those extended families encouraged by Vonnegut, we should also be vigilant in our skepticism of all organizations with ulterior motives tied to monetary wealth or power. The worst form of organization allows the elite to use the masses solely for their own benefit: "The unequal distribution of wealth and its harmful influence on American society and culture is one of Vonnegut's most important recurring themes" (Marvin, 2002, p. 19).

Materialism and capitalism

Probably the quality in Vonnegut the man and the artist that places him most out of sync with his modern audience and his fellow Americans is his rejection of the value of materialism and the great promise of capitalism. His work certainly is informed by his experiences as a young writer who found some wealth and success early as a writer of short stories and his eventual need to work at GE and even as a Saab salesman. The need to earn money plagued much of his early adult life and stood in direct contrast to his artistic drive. *Player Piano* captures some of that distrust in materialism and capitalism, and then in *Bluebeard,* he more directly explores the corrupting influence of capitalism as it impacts not only the individual but also the entire world of art. Just as I would not imply that Vonnegut is suggesting we abandon technology, I would also not imply that Vonnegut wishes America would abandon capitalism. He is clearly arguing, however, that we have a warped sense of proportion. Modern Americans are blindly driven to acquire more and more stuff merely to acquire more and more stuff, particularly to the exclusion of pursuing anything else of value in our brief existences. In the "Prologue" to *Jailbird,* Vonnegut (1979) states that all of his work could have been (should have been) replaced by a "seven-word telegram" he received from a high school student, "'Love may fail, but courtesy will prevail'" (p. 2). Vonnegut and many critics have also captured the essential Vonnegut message as the Golden Rule. This seems fair, and that materialism and capitalism corrupt our drive to do unto others is probably his actual distrust of both.

Behavioral psychology

Vonnegut's concern for science generally is associated with technology, but many of his works address the powerful hold behavioral psychology has on numerous aspects of American life. In *Player Piano,* for example, IQ testing and the subtle manipulation of stimulus/response techniques inherent in the business world are attacked directly. In the early twentieth century, the research and theories of B.F. Skinner, Pavlov, and others established themselves in our public education system and eventually in our business and industry paradigms. Over the last half of the 1900s, many began to identify the essentially mechanistic nature of behavioral psychology *in its application*. Vonnegut has IQ testing determine each person's entire career and life in *Player Piano* as a warning to the indirect ways in which IQ and other such educational testing impact most Americans today. When we expose our students to analyzing behavioral psychology in our culture and how it manifests itself in Vonnegut's work, we must be careful to help students distinguish between how behaviorism looks in practice and in theory; few would argue, for instance, that behaviorists *desire* the mechanistic and dehumanizing results of their science that Vonnegut exposes.

Freethinking, socialism, and humanism

"I am in fact pretty much an Atheist like my mother's father, although I kept that to myself. Why argue somebody else out of the expectation of some sort of Afterlife?" confesses Eugene Debs Hartke in *Hocus Pocus,* who is named after Eugene Victor Debs, "a Socialist and a Pacifist and a Labor Organizer who ran several times for the Presidency of the United States of America" (p. 1). This fictional confession is paralleled with Vonnegut's many pronouncements concerning his own agnosticism/atheism, socialistic tendencies, and passivism—pronouncements that are often ironically punctuated with references to Jesus. "'I am enchanted by the Sermon on the Mount,'" begins what Vonnegut lists as a "sermon" ("Palm Sunday") in the collection *Palm Sunday* (p. 296). This concluding piece in that book captures the many twists and turns of Vonnegut's mind, a mind that embraces passionately the central tenants of love and devotion found in Jesus' words while rejecting the religion (and even God) founded in His name. Ultimately, Vonnegut argues in his fiction and nonfiction that a freethinker, a socialist, and a humanist are the most *humane* things he can be, and the most humane things anyone can be. He makes these arguments in a culture that has primarily demonized all of those terms—possibly beyond repair. Since, as his narrator in *Hocus Pocus* states, Vonnegut has never seemed to be interested in converting anyone to any movement, we have to believe that Vonnegut genuinely wishes to use his perspective to bring his readers and audiences to a state of consideration and reconsideration.

Art

"[H]ere is my picture of an asshole," greets the reader of *Breakfast of Champions* early in the novel, followed immediately by Vonnegut's now famous but crude drawing referred to as an asterisk (p. 5). Similar crude drawings populate this novel, and in classic Vonnegut fashion, his artwork confronts the reader with an odd combination of innocence and profanity that we find in his narratives. By the publication of *Bluebeard,* we see that Vonnegut has a serious interest in the entire world of art, the nature of art, and the state of art within a capitalistic paradigm. "For Vonnegut, art does not possess intrinsic value; rather, it refers to humanity's intrinsic value," explains David

Andrews (Boon, 2001, p. 19). Vonnegut cares deeply for the sanctity of our humanity, and he sees that the highest goal of art is to reinforce that sanctity. "This is how art should work," adds Andrews, "but what Vonnegut and *Bluebeard* do best is dissect the various historical processes that corrupt art"—and we might add, humanity (Boon, p. 19). Vonnegut's own art as a writer and as a visual artist attempts to embody what he believes all art should do—that which is best for the human race.

War and peace

Most people who know of Vonnegut's work associate him with *Slaughterhouse-Five;* from that single association, his work appears to be about war. If Vonnegut is too often pigeon-holed as a writer of science fiction, he may just as well be too often described as a war novelist. A more fair assessment of Vonnegut is that he detests war; his works are the commentary of a passivist, a man who has lived through WWII as a POW in one of the most dramatic events of war, the firebombing of Dresden. By the time Vonnegut could fully explore that experience in *Slaughterhouse-Five,* the U.S. was divided and fighting on the home front over the conflict known as Vietnam. The novel, in essence, stands as a protest to *that* war—and *all* war—since Vonnegut believes that humanity's propensity for war is one of our flaws that will bring about that end of times about which humans also fight. "Vonnegut continues to crusade in both his fiction and his nonfiction for a world where humans can love and care for one another," Davis notes (Boon, 2001, p. 160). For Vonnegut, war of any kind is the ultimate corruption of that world.

Religion

"'I suggest that we need a new religion,'" Vonnegut (1981) declares, later adding, "'If I have offended anyone here by talking of the need of a new religion, I apologize. I am willing to drop the word religion, and substitute for it these three words: *heartfelt moral code*'" (pp. 181, 184). The complaint about religion in Vonnegut seems to be about the organization of religion, not the broad moral messages housed in any religion. Davis (Boon, 2001) verifies that Vonnegut "attempts to retell old, but useful, stories. . . . In the retelling, however, there can be no dogmatism, no reestablishment of a fixed center" (p. 160). That moral codes often serve as the bricks to build religions that turn those codes into dogmatic weapons used to oppress humanity disturbs Vonnegut greatly. His books, notably *Cat's Cradle,* ask readers to set aside the dogmatism and embrace instead heartfelt moral codes that can be found quite easily in the words of Jesus.

American popular culture

I have argued elsewhere (Thomas, 2004) that America is unique in its commitment to a narrow sense of science and religion while simultaneously believing that science and religion are in direct contradiction to each other. Vonnegut's work addresses again and again these American paradoxes and hypocrisies—conflicts of science and religion, of religion and war, of capitalism and human dignity. Vonnegut opens *Breakfast of Champions* by acknowledging that his novel's title echoes "a registered trademark of General Mills, Inc."; he goes on to say that he doesn't suggest any association with the company or "[intend] to disparage their fine products" (p. 1). Later, the narrator mentions the U.S., and adds, "This was their national anthem, which was pure balderdash, like so much they were expected to take seriously" (p. 7). And the reader soon realizes that Vonnegut plans to uncover and criticize much of what America holds valuable, including major corporations, hollow slogans, and the American Dream. However, such criticisms are never intended to tear down the country. On the contrary, Vonnegut belongs to a tradition that sets out to criticize in order to improve. This distinction has often been lost when we believe that in order to survive that this country must speak with one voice during world wars, the McCarthy Era, post-9/11 America, etc.

Free will

Midway through *Slaughterhouse-Five,* a Tralfamadorian says to Billy Pilgrim, "'Only on Earth is there any talk of free will'" (p. 109). Whether directly stated or implicit in his stories, the debate about whether humans have free will pervades Vonnegut's writing. Nearly thirty years later, Vonnegut writes in *Timequake,* "I asked the late great German novelist Heinrich Boll what the basic flaw was in the German character. He said, 'Obedience'" (p. 42). Vonnegut seems to wrestle throughout his career with the apparent fact that humans do *not* have free will, yet the basic quality he wishes to preserve in humanity is our ability to live *as if* we have free will—resisting the pressures placed upon us to be obedient, compliant. This conflict within Vonnegut's work is a theme that is most likely to resonate with young people since they often find themselves in the cusp of that same dilemma.

Humanity's tragic flaw and the end of time

In a brilliant array of scenarios, Vonnegut time and again plays with humanity bringing about the end of the world as we know it;

"a major theme in Vonnegut's fiction [is] ... the possibility that man has a tragic flaw that relentlessly moves him in the direction of self-annihilation" (Schatt, 1976, p. 28). Addressing the end of time is risky business for an author who is openly critical of fundamentalist cries about the Apocalypse; so we have to see that Vonnegut tends to look closely at how we are conducting ourselves as humans *now* and then constructs his version of the worst case scenario from that behavior through his fiction. In essence, Vonnegut hopes to educate us so that we can avoid our tragic flaws more so than he attempts to draw any real picture of how this planet or all of humanity *will* end. Readers of science fiction seem to revel in stories that look back at today from the vantage point of post-Apocalyptic civilizations. Vonnegut manipulates that standard element of the science fiction genre in his works aimed at a wider reading public.

The topics and thematic concerns outlined above allow any reader, student, or teacher to approach a Vonnegut work with a framework of expectations, but we all have to expect the unexpected with Vonnegut. The art in Vonnegut is that he evolves in his concern for these topics over his career and even within single works. Vonnegut's essential messages never change dramatically, but he is nearly as intent on emphasizing the complexity of these issues as he is to offer his perspectives.

Craft of a Freethinker

Marvin (2002) explains, "At different stages of his career, Kurt Vonnegut's writing has been categorized as science fiction, satire, black humor, and postmodern" (p. 13). Vonnegut as a craftsperson deals with the above topics and themes within frameworks, such as the four noted by Marvin. Here, we will briefly explore how Vonnegut's work can be categorized while also suggesting that his work simultaneously fits and contradicts these classifications.

Player Piano established Vonnegut as a science fiction writer because his early work is "set in the future and included space ships, super computers, and other technological gadgets" (Marvin, 2002, p. 13). Vonnegut simultaneously rejects being labeled as a science fiction writer while continuing to fill his work with futuristic settings and as much technology and science as a work can hold. Ultimately, the reader begins to see that "Vonnegut uses the conventions of science fiction to force his readers to think more deeply about the world we actually live in," explains Marvin (p. 14). Other writers of serious fiction have also found themselves associated with science fiction, such as Aldous Huxley and George Orwell; yet, most serious writers of science fiction—Arthur C. Clark, Isaac Asimov, Ray

Bradbury—have been relegated to being mere genre writers and afforded the same sort of minimal respect as Stephen King or Anne Rice. For students and teachers, asking whether or not Vonnegut is a science fiction writer is a valuable pursuit for the classroom—along with arguing whether or not Vonnegut is an author on the same level as American novelists Faulkner, Fitzgerald, Steinbeck, and Hemingway.

ENTRY POINT

Vonnegut confronts science fiction in the opening essay of *Wampeters, Foma & Granfalloons,* "Science Fiction." Klinkowitz (1998) feels that this essay "serves well as an introduction to Kurt Vonnegut, person and writer" (p. 61). Students often develop a flat sense of genre as a direct result of the stilted nature of the traditional canon. Their reading list has little variety and consists almost exclusively of *serious* works; there is no room for genre fiction and humor in most English courses. After viewing a *Star Trek* episode or a 1950s science fiction movie such as *Invasion of the Body Snatchers,* students can be asked to develop characteristics of what distinguishes science fiction from other subgenres. A "What is science fiction?" entry point can establish a frame of reference both for the conventions used by Vonnegut in his work and for Vonnegut's tendency to satirize those conventions while implementing them.

If any quality of Vonnegut as a craftsperson deserves emphasis it is his ability as a satirist. Vonnegut sees anything as a target for his critical humor. Marvin (2002) believes "Vonnegut's humor forces readers to confront the pain and suffering that humans inflict on one another" (p. 15). The students who are confronted by Vonnegut's often stark satire—especially his targeting of ideas and people that many young people have been taught to accept somewhat blindly out of respect—are well acquainted with satire from their lives spent with television (such as *Saturday Night Live* and *The Daily Show with Jon Stewart*), but they often flounder when dealing with the printed word. Teachers need to help students make that transition in their sensitivity to satire. Vonnegut's work as a satirist, as with his science fiction leanings, creates yet another reason for critics to marginalize his work. Satirists often do "not create well-rounded characters.... Instead [they make] fun of recognizable human types" (Marvin, p. 15). Vonnegut's satire, then, is quite effective in the English classroom as we explore the development of characters. For the satirist, characterization is often a technique that is a means to a greater end—the critical uncovering of some idea, behavior, or person.

ENTRY POINT AND CONNECTIONS

Marvin (2002) offers *The Simpsons* as an ideal entry point for discussing satire and, thus, Vonnegut. This cartoon has many of the highest qualities of satire, but it also serves well students who might be uncomfortable with satire that cuts into topics and beliefs that have remained untouched in their lives. *The Simpsons*, like Vonnegut, takes a sharp knife to religion, for instance, while maintaining the ability to offer messages that we can easily label as moral. Once students feel comfortable with satire as a form and as a technique, a unit with multiple satirical works may be very effective. Combining a Vonnegut novel with Jonathan Swift's *Gulliver's Travels* and Aldous Huxley's *Brave New World* provides students with a broad base of satire over a long period of literature. Hartley S. Spatt notes "[t]he novels written during the first half of Vonnegut's career fall into the American tradition of social satire" (Boon, 2001, p. 127); a unit such as the one noted here can show students how Vonnegut fits into the American tradition of satire as well as the larger tradition American literature owes to our British roots.

Literary humor is often satirical, but it also tends to fall into a category called "black," "dark," or "grotesque" humor. My students were often puzzled by the ability or even need for authors to juxtapose tragedy and comedy, such as the many humorous yet violent scenes in the works of Flannery O'Connor. Vonnegut clearly relies on the techniques of dark humorists. His *Slaughterhouse-Five* raises humor out of the ashes of a great horror of war—and not just any war. WWII and the reign of Hitler and his massacre of millions of Jews certainly do not seem appropriate topics for bringing a reader to laughter. "Laughter and tears are both responses to frustration and exhaustion, to the futility of thinking and striving anymore. I myself prefer to laugh, since there is less cleaning up to do afterward—and since I can start thinking and striving again that much sooner," Vonnegut tells his readers in *Palm Sunday* (p. 298). We might add that he prefers his readers to laugh as well.

CONNECTIONS

A unit on dark humor can be successful, just as a unit on satire can be. Marvin (2002) places Vonnegut in the same dark humor vein as Terry Southern's *Dr. Strangelove*, John Barth's *The Floating Opera*, and Joseph Heller's *Catch-22*. A work such as *Slapstick* could be combined with these novels for students to explore dark humor as an effective element of a more broadly painted satire.

One of the complex but significant elements of Vonnegut's works is his own straddling of the modernist and postmodernist eras of literature. Most critics categorize Vonnegut as an experimental and postmodern writer (see Todd F. Davis in Boon, 2001). Davis argues that Vonnegut "is more concerned with our response to existence than with the philosophical nature of that existence" (p. 151). Further, we see that Vonnegut is a relativist; his works directly confront the modernist assumption of objectivity. His relativist nature is at the heart of his skeptical stance toward both science and religion—two aspects of human existence that gravitate toward dogmatism and law.

This initial chapter is intended as an introduction for reading, learning, and teaching the works of Kurt Vonnegut. Vonnegut notes in an address at Wheaton College Library that "William F. Buckley said in a recent column that I would be overjoyed by Nixon's political defeat, since I had made a career of despising America. That proves he hasn't read me much" (*Wampeters, Foma & Granfalloons*, pp. 219–220). I hope that with this book, that anyone reading Vonnegut for any reason can come out the other side of his novels and avoid the mistake made by Mr. Buckley.

FOR FURTHER STUDY-KURT VONNEGUT

Books

Allen, W. R. (1988). *Conversations with Kurt Vonnegut.* Jackson: University Press of Mississippi.

"These interviews reveal that Vonnegut began more as a scientist than a novelist," explains Allen in the volume's introduction (p. ix). This is an excellent collection and a unique source of Vonnegut interviews. Notable in this collection is the often-mentioned *Playboy* interview with Vonnegut.

Allen, W. R. (1991). *Understanding Kurt Vonnegut.* Columbia: University of South Carolina Press.

Like other volumes in this series, this critical introduction to Vonnegut is excellent for teachers and students because it is comprehensive and highly accessible for both students and teachers who are looking for the essential responses to Vonnegut's work. While the volume focuses primarily on Vonnegut as a novelist, it does include a very useful bibliography and will serve as a solid entry point into exploring Vonnegut critically.

Boon, K. A., ed. (2001). *At millennium's end: New essays on the work of Kurt Vonnegut.* Albany, NY: State University of New York Press.

This collection of critical essays offers the most up-to-date assessment of Vonnegut available. The essays are highly accessible and excellent both for teachers and students. Since these essays do a wonderful job of capturing the entire span of Vonnegut's works and the critical and popular reactions to those works, this is a necessary resource when dealing with Vonnegut.

Klinkowitz, J. (1990). Slaughterhouse-Five: *Reforming the novel and the world.* Boston: Twayne Publishers.

Slaughterhouse-Five is arguably Vonnegut's most important work; it is easily his most read and studied work. This critical analysis, then, is an essential resource for teachers or students dealing with his first critically acknowledged work. Klinkowitz provides a comprehensive exploration of the novel along with a detailed chronology of Vonnegut's life and works. In the opening three chapters, Klinkowitz provides a solid foundation for the reader, detailing the historical context of the novel, the critical value of the novel, and its initial reception. The following four chapters are a thorough analysis of the novel. This volume is more than a critical analysis of a novel, however; Klinkowitz offers a solid consideration of both criticism of literature and the nature of novel and genre forms.

Klinkowitz, J. (1998). *Vonnegut in fact: The public spokesmanship of personal fiction.* Columbia: University of South Carolina Press.

This critical exploration of Vonnegut focuses heavily on the nonfiction tendency of Vonnegut's fiction and the fictional aspects of Vonnegut the essayist and speech writer. Klinkowitz is one of the top Vonnegut scholars, and his discussion here is valuable for teachers and students who wish to consider the essential nature of Vonnegut the writer and Vonnegut the spokesperson. This volume considers three of Vonnegut's collections of nonfiction—*Wampeters, Foma & Granfalloons, Palm Sunday,* and *Fates Worse than Death.* As well, this analysis of Vonnegut provides an excellent foundation for exploring the nature of genre.

Marvin, T. F. (2002). *Kurt Vonnegut: A critical companion.* Westport, CT: Greenwood Press.

This stands as the most current book-length discussion of Vonnegut you can find. The books in this series are extremely helpful and comprehensive. This volume includes full chapters on *Player Piano, The Sirens of Titan, Mother Night, Cat's Cradle, God Bless You, Mr. Rosewater, Slaughterhouse-Five,* and *Bluebeard* along with chapters on his life and the major motifs of his work.

Merrill, R., ed. (1990). *Critical essays on Kurt Vonnegut.* Boston: G. K. Hall and Company.

This collection of critical discussions of Vonnegut's work is notable for its inclusion of reviews, criticism of the early works, three considerations of *Slaughterhouse-Five,* criticism of Vonnegut's later works, and two general studies. These critical collections from Hall are valuable resources for both advanced students and teachers who are dealing with Vonnegut's works. The collection of reviews can serve as models for students who are exploring writing critical book reviews and may be paired with Vonnegut's own unique approach to reviewing books.

Morse, D. E. (2003). *The novels of Kurt Vonnegut: Imagining being an American.* Westport, CT: Praeger.

"The emphasis of this study falls, therefore, on the value of reading Vonnegut's novels, their relation to American experience, and their distinguishing features as fiction," explains Morse in his Preface (p. xiii). Morse focuses this study on Vonnegut's work from *Player Piano* through *Timequake* as those books fit into an American tradition typified by the works of Emerson, Thoreau, and Twain. Particularly for teachers of American literature, Morse's introduction and the following chapters characterize American literature as found in Emerson, Thoreau, and Twain as well as defining Vonnegut in those terms, essentially offering a scholarly argument for Vonnegut as a valuable part of the American literary canon (and not simply a writer of science fiction).

Mustazza, L., ed. (1994). *The critical response to Kurt Vonnegut.* Westport, CT: Greenwood Press.

Divided into two parts of roughly twenty years each in the career of Kurt Vonnegut, this collection assembles book reviews and critical essays on Vonnegut's novels from *Player Piano* in 1952 through *Hocus Pocus* in the early 1990s. The collection is valuable as both a timeline and a barometer of how readers, reviewers, and critics responded to Vonnegut over forty years of his publishing novels. For students and teachers, this collection organizes several reviews and critical essays per novel in one volume, aiding scholarship on most of his works.

Reed, P. J., & Leeds, M., eds. (1996). *The Vonnegut chronicles: Interviews and essays.* Westport, CT: Greenwood Press.

This collection offers some material more recent than Allen's collection of Vonnegut interviews. The contents offer three interviews not in the Allen collection along with eleven critical essays; also included are an essay on Vonnegut as a graphic artist and a selected bibliography covering 1985–1994.

Schatt, S. (1976). *Kurt Vonnegut.* Boston: Twayne Publishers.

This is a traditional and accessible critical discussion of Vonnegut from the Twayne series aimed at students. The book only deals with his work up to *Slapstick,* but the analysis is solid and proves helpful to anyone looking for essential information about Vonnegut.

Websites

The Vonnegut Web, Chris Huber, 2005, http://www.vonnegutweb.com/index.html.

While this Web page should be classified as an unofficial Vonnegut site—something of a fan site—it is extremely comprehensive and accurate. It includes a number of valuable internal links such as:

- Biographical Details & Highlights
- Archives—Vonnegut writings from forgotten places
- Chronology—Mapping Vonnegut's life and texts
- Commencement Addresses
- Complete Writings—Novels, short story collections, essays, plays, adaptations

KURT VONNEGUT 31

- Critical Bibliography—A comprehensive bibliography of Vonnegut criticism and sources
- Dramatic Works—Details on *Happy Birthday, Wanda June, Between Time & Timbuktu, L'Histoire du Soldat* and more
- Education—The higher education of Kurt Vonnegut
- Family Background—Details on brother Bernard, uncle Alex, wife Jill Krementz, son Mark, and more
- Formal Honors—Honorary degrees, awards
- Frequently Asked Questions—The official FAQ for alt.books.kurt-vonnegut
- Interests—A few of Vonnegut's pursuits
- Interviews—Chats ranging between 1974–2002
- Kilgore Trout—A home page for the prolific sci-fi writer
- Linkography—Selected links to Vonnegutian pages beyond
- Occupations—How the résumé would look
- Research—Original research on Vonnegut and resources for writing on Vonnegut.

The Official Website of Kurt Vonnegut, 2002, http://www.vonnegut.com.

It includes basic links: "Bio," "Books," "News," "Order," "Screenprints," and "Sculpture." This page is no more than basics, but it offers some opportunities to explore Vonnegut the visual artist; it also is a nice place for serious Vonnegut fans to order T-shirts and Vonnegut artwork. The "News" link does include some nice photographs and links to recent Vonnegut publishings and commentaries—such as pieces written for the progressive journal *In These Times* in 2003 and 2004.

Marek Vit's Kurt Vonnegut Corner, 2002, http://www.geocities.com/Hollywood/4953/vonn.html.

Another comprehensive and informative unofficial site. The links include "About Kurt Vonnegut," "Essay Collection" (primarily pieces written by students, thus a good link to check if you suspect students of plagiarism), "Collection of Quotes," "Kilgore Trout," "Image Gallery," "Miscellaneous," and "Useful Links."

Welcome to the Monkey House . . . or, How Kurt Vonnegut Changed Our Lives, Brian Rodriguez, 2002, http://www.ipass.net/brianrodr/vonnegut/.

This unofficial website has a neat twist; it deals with how Vonnegut has slipped into the work of musicians and into TV and the movies. The links include "Adaptations," "Bands," Links," "Miscellaneous," and "Movies & TV." The comprehensive nature of this website makes it invaluable when teachers and students are searching for anything and everything related to the works of Kurt Vonnegut.

ENTRY POINTS AND CONNECTIONS

Confessions of a Dangerous Mind (2003), George Clooney, director

Confessions of a Dangerous Mind: An Unauthorized Autobiography (1982/2002), Chuck Barris

Lolita, Vladimir Nabokov

The Adventures of Huckleberry Finn, Mark Twain

"Politics and the English Language," George Orwell

Ernest Hemingway

"For Sacco and Vanzetti," Barbara Kingsolver, *Another America*

2001, Arthur C. Clarke (novel), Stanley Kubric, director (movie)

Freethinkers: A History of American Secularism, Susan Jacoby

Star Trek

Invasion of the Body Snatchers

"Science Fiction," Kurt Vonnegut

The Simpsons

Gulliver's Travels, Jonathan Swift

Brave New World, Aldous Huxley

Dr. Strangelove, Terry Southern

The Floating Opera, John Barth

Catch-22, Joseph Heller

Chapter Two

Kurt Vonnegut's Nonfiction Universe

"From all that crap, I have culled this volume"

Although somewhat discounting New Journalism, Vonnegut may be writing here about the false and essentially pointless distinction between fiction and nonfiction as primary parameters for writing genres: "And fiction is melody, and journalism, new or old, is noise" (*Wampeters, Foma & Granfalloons,* p. xviii). Vonnegut seems to return in all of his collections of nonfiction to preferring fiction on all levels and to identifying fictional qualities and techniques that raise nonfiction to fictional heights. This preference for fiction and fictional techniques places Vonnegut squarely in synchronicity with how we approach literature in English classes in high school and college. Students receive direct and indirect arguments that fiction matters most.

Yet, in the world outside of formal schooling, nonfiction of many types dominates our lives. I am suspicious that Vonnegut actually values all writing quite equally, that Vonnegut ultimately finds distinguishing among genres a silly exercise. His work, as we will explore, tends to defy easy labels; his novels drift into autobiography and commentary as his nonfiction is sustained by his greatest fictional techniques such as storytelling.

In this chapter, I will discuss how we can implement Vonnegut's collections of nonfiction—*Wampeters, Foma & Granfalloons, Palm Sunday, Fates Worse than Death,* and *A Man without a Country*—as avenues to enhance our students as both readers and writers of nonfiction. The main divisions of this discussion will focus on nonfiction as a genre, speeches, humor, reviews and Op-Ed essays, and New Journalism.

In *Palm Sunday,* Vonnegut announces, "It is a marvelous new literary form. This book combines the tidal power of a major novel with the bone-rattling immediacy of front-line journalism" (p. xi). I maintain that this pronouncement is valid for virtually all of Vonnegut's nonfiction, making those works ideal for our classrooms as we confront our students with ideas that are "bone rattling" and encourage them to express themselves through language in equally impressive ways.

Considering and Reconsidering Nonfiction as a Genre

If we ask students at the secondary or college level to tell us what nonfiction is, we are likely to encounter a typical student urge to recall a definition provided to them somewhere in their English education. The student brave enough to tackle the question will probably spout something like, "It's true," followed soon after (if we make no response) by, "Or not true—it's one of those, but I can never remember."

A common but flawed urge of any teacher is to make new learning as simple as possible for students; the result of such an approach is that we often reduce authentic learning to simplistic rote memorization that actually causes more misunderstanding than understanding. Helping students distinguish between fiction and nonfiction as genres is one of the most fertile areas for such a mistake. Traditionally, students are often taught the terms "fiction" and "nonfiction" by the definition approach first, possibly followed by exploring models of the forms. Those definitions tend to portray fiction as "not true" and nonfiction as "true."

Since we encounter students in high school and college who already have these misleading definitions burned into their minds, we can address nonfiction as a genre by first attacking student misconceptions and oversimplified definitions. I have found that discussions of genre have to be preceded by discussions of "truth." I make a distinction with my students between little "t" truth and big "T" Truth—connecting that distinction with more complex definitions of fiction and nonfiction. We note that little "t" truth denotes those things we may label as facts—such as "Gas costs $2.85 at that station" or "Thomas Jefferson founded the University of Virginia." With "truth" we are identifying the things of our temporal life that can be verified through observation of some kind. Big "T" Truth connotes the larger ideas that humanity tends to accept as universally valid—such as "Do unto others as you would have them do unto you." With "Truth" we are dealing in the larger ideas, and thus we are moving into a realm that is debatable (unlike "truth") and beyond simple observation of phenomena.

We have no reason to debate the current price for gas at a local station, but we can and probably even should argue about the meaning of life or the nature of romantic love. This distinction provides a basis for redefining "fiction" and "nonfiction." I ask students to consider that writers of *both* fiction and nonfiction are ultimately concerned with Truth. The avenues for approaching Truth, however, differ for writers of fiction and nonfiction. Fiction writers use *created* avenues to pursue Truth (created characters and plots); nonfiction writers use fact (that which is *true,* as in the details of the writer's life, statistics, or history) to pursue Truth.

The dilemma created by reconsidering genre (which we will discuss later in this chapter and throughout this book) is the postmodern argument that we can never truly capture that which is true or factual because we necessarily distort once we recreate. Part of the instructional value of dealing extensively with nonfiction is this debate. Students must begin to consider whether the writing about facts is not essentially fictional writing since we are *recreating* people and events.

One effective entry point for this tension between modernism and postmodernism can be found in reading and writing biography, memoirs, and autobiography. I was fortunate to write for my dissertation a biography of an English educator, Lou LaBrant. This experience of researching biography as a field and of writing a biography allows me to share with students the interpretive and creative nature of composing nonfiction. I also began to discuss with students the existence of and need to create multiple biographies of the same person—noting the large number of biographies of Thomas Jefferson. While pursuing fact certainly impacts a writer, while attempting to be accurate greatly impacts a writer, we must recognize that nonfiction writing necessarily distorts details even in the hands of the most conscientious writer.

CONNECTION

Jerome Klinkowitz (Boon, 2001) notes that "[i]n *Timequake*, novel and essay are united in a new form by which the author presents neither fiction nor nonfiction, but rather the autobiography of a novel" (p. 14). To have students explore the overlapping qualities of fiction and nonfiction in works separated by about 150 years, *Timequake* can be paired with Henry David Thoreau's *Walden*—a work that has often defied a simple label since Thoreau wrote an essentially true account of his time at Walden Pond, while taking many liberties with facts and incorporating techniques often associated with fiction. These works provide rich opportunities to discuss genre while exploring the nature of writing across the relatively brief history of American literature. Vonnegut and Thoreau also stand as distinct from each other yet unique American voices, writers and thinkers who speak and spoke against the popular beliefs and practices of their days.

- -

Vonnegut's writing proves to be ideal for asking students to explore genre and the nature of truth—as well as the larger arguments that have grown during the postmodern era. Let's look here at how we can implement Vonnegut's nonfiction essays in our classrooms as avenues to discussing the nature of nonfiction, using his "Brief Encounters on the Inland Waterway" from *Wampeters, Foma & Granfalloons* as an example of the types of approaches we can use with virtually any of his pieces. Through this essay, students can build or expand their understanding of reading nonfiction and essay writing, of the techniques and characteristics of nonfiction, of the need to have prior knowledge of the facts to fully appreciate nonfiction, of the use of literary allusion in nonfiction, of the craft involved in manipulating syntax and tone in nonfiction, and of the use of humor in nonfiction.

"Brief Encounters on the Inland Waterway" is a typical Vonnegut "demystification of a another favorite target" (Klinkowitz, 1998, p. 62), political icons in American culture—notably the Kennedys of Hyannis Port. The essay offers the reader Vonnegut's own experience on the Kennedy yacht, the *Marlin*. Klinkowitz explains, "This contrast, between grave significance and frivolous use, structures the entire essay, built as it is on irony that such a famous and expensive ship is hardly ever used by its larger-than-life owners" (p. 63). The essay develops as most of Vonnegut's writing does, broken into brief sections with little or no transitions yet held together ultimately by larger qualities such as his narrative voice.

This essay can serve many instructional purposes:

- Students enter our classes with more problems than simply not knowing how to define genres. Most students have experienced years of writing highly prescribed essays, forms that are often seen only in English classrooms or other academic settings (Thomas, 2005b). One of my primary goals in any English course is to allow students to pursue the most authentic writing forms possible. To achieve that, I believe we must ask students to deconstruct the essay writing of skilled and respected writers (Thomas, 2005a), particularly as a rejection of the traditionally assigned essay form (introduction with overt thesis, sequenced body, and repetitive conclusion). Students should be asked to analyze how Vonnegut begins, develops, and ends "Brief Encounters on the Inland Waterway." The opening is certainly not an introduction and it clearly has no traditional thesis. Instead, Vonnegut opens with four highly detailed paragraphs that are primarily driven by description. Students can be asked to attempt such an opening technique in their own essays, noting that this technique is designed to provide focus and create reader engagement, more authentic in its form and intent than the artificial thesis sentence. Further, students should be able to see that this essay is driven by narration, a technique they tend to associate with fiction. Vonnegut's works often manipulate the orthodox use of linear narration, again a valuable opportunity to discuss narrative techniques. This essay also contradicts the traditional use of the redundant academic conclusion. An effective question to pose for students is, "How does Vonnegut provide the reader with an ending that is satisfying?" This question is loaded—the assumption that the ending *is* satisfying—and instructional—the assertion that the primary purpose in essay is to satisfy the reader (not to restate the introduction and thesis in different words).

- Regardless of the text being read, readers' understanding is greatly impacted by how the content of the text (and the writer's mind) matches the content of the reader's mind. For students I often draw a triangle with "Reader," "Writer," and "Text" at each angle and with "Teacher/Authority" or "Culture" labeling a space encircling the triangle. The diagram is intended to illustrate for students the complex nature of making meaning through text for both readers and writers. To understand "Brief Encounters on the Inland Waterway," contemporary students need to have some of the same knowledge of the Kennedy family of American lore that Vonnegut addresses in his essay. Teachers can provide some of that directly or through having students research the Kennedy family before reading the essay. Above all else, we must be certain to emphasize the need for students to seek information that will fill in gaps in their prior knowledge to become more effective readers of nonfiction.

CONNECTION

One of the most disturbing and debated moments of modern American mythology concerns the event often referred to as Chappaquiddick. At the nexus of America's turbulent 1960s and 1970s, Ted Kennedy stood at the center of a mysterious and unsolved death involving a young woman who drowned in the car Kennedy drove off a bridge into Poucha Pond. Joyce Carol Oates wrote a haunting novel, *Black Water,* that fictionalizes this low point in the mythology of America's Kennedy dynasty. Students often are fascinated by this incident, although many have little or no knowledge of the accident or the unresolved debate over Ted Kennedy's culpability in the woman's death. Oates's novel is a wonderful connection to building student knowledge about the Kennedy family and the role they have played in recent American politics, included the ironic connection existing recently with Maria Shriver (a member of the Kennedy family) as first lady of California with the election of Arnold Schwarzenegger as a Republican. The qualities of Oates's novel also fit well into the discussion of truth and Truth, of fiction and nonfiction, and of narrative techniques and conventions that students are considering while reading Vonnegut.

- -

- Students tend to form neat and inaccurate associations: Alliteration is a technique found only in poetry, or literary allusion is something dead white male authors do in their fiction and poetry so teachers can tell students what literature really means. In "Brief Encounters on the Inland Waterway," Vonnegut offers, "Call me Molly Bloom. Call me Ishmael" (p. 8) and "For the first time, it is possible to have the fantasy of being Huck Finn" (p. 16). There is a different set of expectations of the reader than mere historical knowledge. These literary allusions demand a fairly narrow knowledge of modern works and authors—James Joyce, Herman Melville, Mark Twain. When we allow literary techniques to become the goal of instruction in English classes, we can often slip into asking students to use literature as a "literary technique hunt," as if identifying a passage as a certain technique is a valuable activity in and of itself (which it isn't). The discussion of literary allusion in Vonnegut's essay, then, can serve two instructional purposes. First, it expands student awareness of the techniques that *all* writers employ in *all* types of writing, thus expanding their expectations as readers and their toolbox of techniques as emerging writers. Second, we must emphasize for students that techniques employed by writers are ways to enhance their messages. Literary allusions are not sprinkled throughout a text so readers can play a sort of game show whereby they shout out, "Molly Bloom is a character in James Joyce's *Ulysses!*" Instead, students should be asked *how* the literary allusion supports the message, the narrative, or the tone of the essay by the brief reference. As Klinkowitz (1998) has noted, Vonnegut's use of relatively narrow literary allusions in an essay about yachting may serve as one of many contrasts between disproportionate things running throughout the essay. Certainly, such literary allusions can provide opportunities for prodding students to expand their reading base if they do not recognize the references.

- A technique more commonly associated with fiction but vital in Vonnegut's essay is dialogue. The essay ends with dialogue:

    "First," said Gunther, "get yourself a yacht." (p. 20)

    The use of dialogue in nonfiction, as with literary allusion, expands student expectations as readers and writer, but it also allows teachers and students to continue their discussion of truth and recreating facts. Most nonfiction dialogue may be classified as *essentially* accurate; many writers of memoir and biography are able to recreate dialogue that is close to the original, but writers often have no exact transcript of all dialogue they wish to include. Nonfiction writers are morally obligated to be as accurate as possible with the use of dialogue; in journalism, we tend to expect verbatim quotes can be verified by meticulous notes or by recordings, for example. But memoir writers and biographers tend to recreate dialogue that captures the nature of conversations while failing to provide the exact words of that discussion. This topic can lead students to debate whether this is appropriate, and it can lead to asking students to work with dialogue in their own essays—writing exercises that require them to record comments during an interview, include direct quotes in their essays, and recreate conversations from their own lives while exploring how to capture what people have said without a transcript or recording as evidence. Students can first be asked to choose people as subjects for close listening in order to identify speech patterns that make each person unique. As writers, students then have to recreate dialogue that exhibits those patterns.

- A few pages into the essay, Frank tells Vonnegut that the yacht was getting "'better than a mile to the gallon'" of gasoline (p. 12). It shocks Vonnegut to learn that the mileage is considered good by Frank. This very brief section demonstrates Vonnegut's use of details as sources of his implications and his tone. The trip by yacht to West Palm consumes 1522 gallons of gas. Vonnegut clearly expects the reader to begin at least to question the extravagance of wealth that exists within not only a family such as the Kennedys but also those surrounding the family. Vonnegut never directly condemns the exuberance of wealth, but the brief dialogue between Frank and Vonnegut about the exact amount of gas used for this pleasure trip is clearly loaded and clearly critical. Depending on the sophistication (as a reader) of the students or the students' own socioeconomic backgrounds, making accurate inferences from this section and being sensitive to Vonnegut's tone can prove to be quite difficult. Again we might ask students to return to the triangle representing the three primary elements in gaining meaning from text and consider the assumptions and frames of reference among writers and readers—and how those assumptions are portrayed in writing. Just as more and more American youth are beginning to see cell phones as a necessity, many young people in our classrooms consume gas rather mindlessly. That perspective makes recognizing Vonnegut's point quite difficult.

- Just as I have noted the artificial nature of essay requirements, I also work to overcome students' equally artificial expectations for paragraphing. Vonnegut's essays tend to model the tendency in newspaper writing toward exceptionally brief paragraphs. I have noticed that formal schooling creates in students a need to create exceptionally long paragraphs. "Brief Encounters on the Inland Waterway" is an excellent model of paragraphing for purpose, especially since it tends to work against traditional dictates of how long paragraphs should be in student writing. In this essay, students can uncover the conventions for paragraphing in dialogue while also exploring how paragraphing affects the rhythm and tone of a narration. The literary allusions mentioned above—"Call me Molly Bloom. Call me Ishmael" (p. 8)—stand as a one-sentence paragraph at the end of one of Vonnegut's sections. Students can be asked how these allusions standing alone as a paragraph impact the essay overall. A natural extension from this reading is encouraging students to experiment with paragraphing in their own essays, looking to see how paragraphing develops their intended rhythm and tone.

- "Throughout ['Brief Encounters on the Inland Waterway'], timing is of the essence, with short paragraphs and single-word sentences set in a rhythm much like that in *Cat's Cradle*," states Jerome Klinkowitz (Boon, 2001, p. 10). The discussions of paragraphing will mesh nicely with discussing tone and the syntactical rhythm Vonnegut creates with his sentence length as well as with his paragraphing. Students can be guided to passages such as, "And it isn't necessary to spend every night in a marina: There is such a thing as an anchor" (p. 13). Simple words along with short sentences and paragraphs are often anathema in English classes at the high school and college levels; thus, students are often intrigued with how published authors work within those parameters while earning praise from their teachers (the same teachers who berate those students for simple vocabulary and short sentences and paragraphs). In fact, I always asked that question directly of my students, acknowledging the contradiction myself. Skilled writers implement simple words and short sentences and paragraphs with *purpose,* of course, distinguishing their writing from novice writers who use simple words and short sentences and paragraphs by default. Once we help students see such a distinction (between purpose and expert use of language as opposed to purposeless and inexpert use of language), they are better equipped to move beyond default writing to purposeful composition.

- Toward the end of Vonnegut's essay, he offers a description of a man who "had blubber hanging all over him" (p. 17). Vonnegut follows that flattering description with "He was grotesquely fat," in case the reader missed the blubber reference. Immediately on the heels of that description, Vonnegut adds a comment by Frank: "'Yachting,' said Frank, with his mouth full, 'isn't really the athletic event some people make it out to be'" (p. 17). Written humor is a gift of Vonnegut's, and he works within a joke-writing tradition that makes many sophisticated readers expect a rim shot after the joke is delivered (we will discuss humor in much greater depth later in this chapter). Novice readers and students often miss this humor since they have a much richer experience of laughing at humor in videos, TV and movies. To make student readers sensitive to humor in texts, we must first tell students that passages are funny; then we must discuss with them why they are humorous.

Having students read virtually any one of Vonnegut's nonfiction works allows them to ponder the large questions of genre, such as what makes nonfiction distinct from fiction—along with how the two approaches overlap. A valuable quality of exploring genre through Vonnegut, I believe, is that the exploration will inevitably leave students with lingering questions, avoiding the tendency of classroom discussion to value solid (and misleading) conclusions over the perpetual uncertainty that accompanies most of the big questions of life.

STUDENT INSIGHT

For freshman students in my ENG 11 course, reading Vonnegut's nonfiction led to their expressing varied and interesting ideas about Vonnegut, his arguments, and about nonfiction. This course used *Palm Sunday* as the anchoring work for our discussion of three Vonnegut novels—*Slaughterhouse-Five, Cat's Cradle,* and *Galapagos.* Here are some reflections on *Palm Sunday* by those freshmen:

I found Vonnegut's overall tone in this chapter [Chapter One] to be a bit more dramatic than necessary, although it did give me a better sense of the importance of what he was saying. Specifically I enjoyed his example of Thomas Aquinas' four laws and the manner in which he both proved a parent's right to protect their child from what they see as evil as well as the need for Americans to retain their rights. I particularly admired the clear way with which he concluded this argument by saying that "our freedom will vanish" if our children grow up practicing divine and natural law as citizens.

Harry Briggs

When I saw the title of the chapter, "Self-Interview," I pictured one man sitting in a small dark room, much like an interrogation room of the FBI. However, as I read more of the details concerning the interview, I began to have another picture—an AOL instant message conversation. The interview itself is full of Vonnegut being random with facts, cynical of the government and world events, and darkly humorous over situations in which he finds himself.

Lauren Young

After reading through Chapter 9 (my designated chapter) of Vonnegut's Palm Sunday, I have come to the conclusion that the man is nuts. Although I do agree with his self promoting statement about him being quite funny. I find that it is rather difficult to be funny on paper. Sure, anyone can crack a joke among friends when the timing is right, but to make the reader laugh out loud is a true talent. There have been few instances in my life when I have started laughing while reading (with the exception of situation circumstances, like the bride catching her hair on fire while walking up the aisle . . . though that's not even that funny). As far as format is concerned, I find that this collection of utter malarkey (if you can call it that, most of what he says is true) is very refreshing. His off-the-wall ramblings, which range from the celebration of puberty to a theory of there being 6 seasons instead of 4, are much more interesting and funnier than 99% of other authors that I have read.

Katherine Varner

From his hairstyle to his writing and all the way to the naming of his first son, Vonnegut tells of the single most influential man that shaped him into the writer he is today. But why is this important to me now? Easy. A valuable lesson can be learned from the actions of Vonnegut, for now it is my turn to act. It is my turn to carry out the process of imitation and thievery, so that I may too, like Vonnegut, (although I seriously doubt to achieve the same amount of success), come into my own as a writer. The ultimate lesson that Vonnegut gives us is that to become a great writer you must imitate the greatest of writers, until the reflection on the paper is not that of someone else, but of your own true style. Thus I will begin this process of imitation by ending my essay. Peace.

West Berry

I hope to one day start my essays as effectively as Vonnegut. Already you can see I need help. It's not just the opening though. He says some things throughout his works that I would love to put in an essay, but I have never had the nerve to be so sincere. This is out of fear of a poor grade.

Brian Emerson

My first reaction to the fourth chapter in Kurt Vonnegut's autobiography Palm Sunday is the memory of a series of conversations I had with a good friend in high school. He was planning on going to medical school and conveyed his fears to me of entry level college science classes that were specifically designed to weed out idiots from the premed program. Vonnegut uses a description of himself as a casualty of his science and anthropology studies to show his movement toward writing. But what engaged me in this chapter were Vonnegut's statements that seem unrelated to his subject matter. His inclusion of his mother's suicide jarred me. While it is clear that Vonnegut's faculty advisor ate cyanide because he was fed up at being unsuccessful in his career pursuits, it is unclear how his mother ties in to this.

Matt Springate

What makes Vonnegut's writing so enjoyable and thus so effective is his remarkable ability to provide his readers with exactly what they do not expect. In the very first question of the interview Vonnegut is asked about serving in World War II. A typical answer might include his division or where he served but Vonnegut, in his infinite ability to defy expectations, has already reached his conclusion while his audience is still waiting for the introduction.

Samantha Hicks

So, my response to "Funnier On Paper Than Most People"? I enjoyed it the first time I read it. Reading the chapter a second time, now with writing in mind, paying more attention to structure and style, I enjoyed it even more. The opening line, "I am better than most people in my trade at making jokes on paper," initially caught me off guard with its apparent self-aggrandizement. Upon finishing the chapter, particularly the second time through, I realized that Vonnegut isn't really boasting—he's joking. He explains near the end of the chapter that he considers himself to be funny not because of any innate talent, but because he feels that he must be funny in order for people to listen to him.

Hank Wynn

Writing to Speak—The "Sweetly Faked Attention" of an Audience

Klinkowitz (1998) believes *"Palm Sunday* displays the presentation talents of a spokesmanship fully formed" (p. 83). Although Vonnegut himself speaks with a great deal of ambiguity about his public speaking career, we will use some speeches preserved in *Palm Sunday* to look at having students both read and write speeches, a form they probably deal with far too seldom in classroom settings. The speech allows teachers to approach a form of nonfiction writing that has many unique features we cannot address with works meant only for the page. Through two of Vonnegut's speeches (and one sermon) in *Palm Sunday,* we will consider the conventions of speeches—notably the commencement address—along with the use of parody to comment on those conventions. Further, we will discuss word choice, tone, and audience as they impact the speech. The provocative topics Vonnegut confronts and his unique perspectives will stimulate students to consider some of the big issues they ultimately must face during the journey from adolescence into adulthood.

"Speaking truthfully is, for Kurt Vonnegut, often a matter of talking plainly," Klinkowitz (1998) explains, providing teachers with a solid foundation for adding the speech to our nonfiction curriculum. When a writer composes a piece to be shared aloud with an audience, the work is significantly impacted by the performance of the speaker and the reactions (or lack thereof) of the audience. In section 11 of *Palm Sunday,* Vonnegut includes two speeches, one a commencement address from 1974 and one a speech from 1980, under the heading of "Religion." Let's discuss these two speeches and follow that by a final discussion of the sermon from which this collection receives its name, "Palm Sunday," in order to find ways to incorporate the study of speeches into our nonfiction curriculum.

"Thoughts of a Free Thinker" was offered as a commencement address at Hobart and Smith Colleges in 1974. Vonnegut begins by discussing the commencement address, typically taking a humorous and critical swipe at the type of speech he will be delivering. We can ask students to look closely at his speech for qualities of parody. Nearly all of Vonnegut's work depends heavily on humor and comic timing. In a speech, that comic timing is more dramatic than in works intended only to be read.

ENTRY POINT

The rhythms and essential qualities of Vonnegut's humor share a striking similarity with the work of writer and director Woody Allen, who began as a standup comic and published a fair amount of written humor in the 1970s.

Klinkowitz (1998) notes the similarity in his discussion of Vonnegut as a nonfiction writer. In *Side Effects,* Woody Allen (1980) includes "My Speech to the Graduates," which opens with a parody of historical crossroads and the need for college graduates to make the right choice of their paths in life. This brief parody of the commencement address is an excellent entry point for looking at Vonnegut's many speeches to college graduates. Allen requires his audience to connect with his references as he wades into the larger concerns of human beings such as science and religion—topics commonly found in Vonnegut's speeches. Allen's writing is an excellent model of the rhythm of speech making as well as the rhythm of humor.

> In our English courses, we endlessly pursue developing in our students a sharp ear for the tone of a text. The spoken word can be massaged in a way that the written word can't, but Vonnegut's speeches come to students on the page, and for them, they will seem little more than nonfiction essays. All writers create tone by their word choice. "Thoughts of a Free Thinker" is classic Vonnegut in that he tends to jostle his audience by shifting the tone of his words within a deeply serious sentence, creating a tension between the topic and the word choice that results in humor and forces the reader to reconsider the topic. At the beginning of this speech, Vonnegut admits that commencement addresses often attempt to impart the meaning of life on the young graduates, but the speaker can only guess: "What are the guesses worth? Scientifically and legally, they are worth doodley-squat" (p. 178). Dropping the level of diction to "doodley-squat" while discussing the meaning of life is a classic Vonnegut technique that he shares with standup comics and humorists. Later in the speech, we get "full of baloney" and "clunker," and here students can distinguish between their own *careless* use of slang and idiomatic language as compared to Vonnegut's *purposeful* use of language that contrasts with the seriousness of his subject. This lesson on the purposeful use of language is one of the essential lessons needed by writers of all ages and experiences.

CONNECTIONS

Many students will have limited experience with speeches in their high school and college English courses. The topics and Vonnegut's perspectives will also challenge many students (particularly those students from relatively conservative backgrounds, which I have dealt with throughout my career in the South). Early in "Thoughts of a Free Thinker," Vonnegut sets up his eventual call for a new religion by noting that "'[w]e know too much for old-time religion; and in a way, that knowledge is killing us'"; later he ponders, "'Can we spit out all our knowledge?'" (p. 182). Students may find these ideas puzzling or intriguing. Regardless of their responses, many students will find two unrelated works engaging as they approach these two ideas in different but interesting ways. Joseph Campbell's interview by Bill Moyers, *The Power of Myth,* is an extended but accessible meditation by Campbell and Moyers concerning modern humans' need to find a new mythology. This interview (available in video formats as well) elaborates Campbell's belief that movies such as *Star Wars* are proof that modern people are seeking new versions of universal truths. Vonnegut's comment about spitting out the knowledge that is killing us may strike students as a truly odd reference, although the concept is common within the major religions. The Garden of Eden myth deals with Adam and Eve being warned about the Tree of Knowledge, for example. A wonderful and intriguing story is J. D. Salinger's "Teddy," which deals with a deeply spiritual boy. Salinger laces the comments by the boy with a number of Eastern concepts, one of which parallels Vonnegut's comment when Teddy mentions vomiting out his knowledge.

- -

The commencement address is followed by Vonnegut's talk commemorating William Ellery Channing on the 200th anniversary of the birth of "a principal founder of Unitarianism in the United States" (p. 192). Both the commencement speech and this talk on Channing share many characteristics of speeches that students should explore as an audience and consider as techniques as they attempt speeches themselves:

- Throughout his speeches, Vonnegut makes a number of references to people and events that require the audience to have extended knowledge of those people and events to grasp fully Vonnegut's points and often his humor. Vonnegut will mention his own creation, Kilgore Trout, as easily as he will O. Henry, Bertrand Russell, the comet Kahoutek, Sacco and Vanzetti, and H. L. Mencken—references that are often completely lost on students today. These references are distinct from allusions in that most of them are temporal, bound by the time, so they are ripe for discussions about the dangers of weighing down one's writing with information that may soon be foreign to your audience. Speeches may not require the writer to consider universality in the same way as essay writing since speeches are short lived by their nature.
- As noted above, both of these speeches provide many models for levels of diction; in the talk about Channing, Vonnegut uses "balderdash" and "goddamned." This use of profanity can be an excellent opportunity to discuss the use of profane language in

nonfiction—as distinct from fiction—particularly concerning the raised danger of using profanity in a speech as the words are spoken and the audience is somewhat captive. Again, this can serve as a discussion of purposefulness of language—as well as a discussion of appropriateness.

- As with fiction, nonfiction in the form of speeches, at the highest level, addresses the larger themes that have interested humans throughout history. Vonnegut is a big idea writer and speaker. Students will be interested in debating and considering those big ideas; the sources of those discussions coming from nonfiction can be an added layer to those debates. Does it matter that Vonnegut's speeches clearly and rather bluntly assert his personal views (in contrast to a writer's fiction that may weave a variety of perspectives within a work, making it difficult to connect those ideas directly with the writer)?

CONNECTION

In his speech about Channing, Vonnegut argues that "'[w]e might also say that one human being is no human being'" (p. 196) as part of his call for renewing folk societies, extended families. In his disturbing and complex short story "Redemption," John Gardner dramatizes that argument as the reader watches a twelve-year-old accidentally run over and kill his younger brother, an event that devastates an entire family. Vonnegut's call for extended families carries with it his own warnings about the positive and negative qualities of families; Gardner's story uncovers similar qualities that are heightened for the Hawthorn family by the death of the child David.

Ultimately, the speeches of Vonnegut provide students with a different nonfiction form within the traditional canon of works in our English classes. The speeches also show students the possibility of weaving larger considerations into personal stories and the events of their worlds—just as Vonnegut does. To expand this experience even further, let's now look at Vonnegut's own sermon—a form of speech that should resonate to some degree with most students although, again, the form is primarily absent from the works we discuss in our classes.

Vonnegut titles his second nonfiction collection from its final essay, "Palm Sunday," a sermon he delivered in 1980. The sermon as a speech is unique in its religious purpose, its textual grounding, and its context primarily being a church or similar religious setting. Vonnegut delivering a sermon offers an odd twist; as he notes in his final comments in "Thoughts of a Free Thinker": "'And now you have just heard an atheist thank God not once, but twice'" (p. 191). In this sermon, Vonnegut calls himself a "Christ-worshipping agnostic," but the contrast between his faith (or lack thereof) and his giving a sermon is an interesting source of classroom discussions. This contrast, however, I believe, makes Vonnegut's sermon ideal for the classroom as his example opens the door for students of all faiths and religions to feel free to write their own sermons from whatever religious texts they prefer. Let's look here at some lessons we can draw from "Palm Sunday":

- Vonnegut chooses to quote from the Revised Standard Version of the Bible since "[t]he funniest joke in the world, if told in King James English, is doomed to sound like Charlton Heston" (p. 297). During our study of *The Scarlet Letter,* I always had students bring their Bibles for group activities dealing with biblical allusions in the novel (please note that I was teaching in the South and virtually 100% of my students were fundamentalist Christians; however, I acknowledged the possibility of students not being Christian and framed the activity in the context of the novel's writer *assuming* his readers have complex knowledge of the Christian Bible). I have found that students are fairly ignorant of translations and various versions of texts originally in languages other than English. Vonnegut briefly notes the problems with translations in his sermon. For students, the dangers and challenges of translation are wonderful issues to be discussed in our English classes.
- Since sermons tend to draw their primary support from religious text, students can gain valuable lessons in quoting and properly interpreting decontextualized quotes—skills valuable to students in the academic world, where support and fair use of textual quotes are required. Vonnegut reads from and interprets John 12, but in Vonnegut's world his sermons weave nonreligious perspectives with religious texts along with finding humor (or creating humor) in the words of Jesus.
- In our English courses, we are and should be responsible for exposing our students to a variety of perspectives; we also need to be sure to model sincere respect for those various perspectives. How then do we bring a Christian sermon into our classrooms for study? Sermons by their nature work within assumptions that the religious text and the audience embrace a set of essential beliefs. Students can use this context to consider how *all* writing functions within a similar context. Writers and their audiences share assumptions and prior knowledge, and writers and their audiences have conflicting or disjointed assumptions and prior knowledge.

All of these dynamics are vital to the success of a sermon—or any purposeful writing.

- In a more narrow consideration, we can use the sermon to ask students to focus on the importance of "audience" in any writing. Vonnegut ends his sermon with, "'I thank you for your sweetly faked attention'" (p. 300). The juxtaposition of "sweetly" with "faked" highlights in a truly succinct emphasis any writer's or speaker's need to engage the audience along with the captive nature of a congregation (or any audience of a speech) as opposed to readers, who are far more free to stop reading.

While I believe adding speeches and the sermon to our classrooms is valuable for expanding our students as readers and thinkers, I see this as primarily a writing unit, leading to students writing and performing their own speeches. A writing assignment that involves students giving their speeches would certainly be time intensive. If presenting the speeches one at a time is impossible, we can consider putting students in groups of three to five students and having them deliver their speeches only to those small groups to save time. An added feature of this assignment can be designing assessment rubrics (with the students involved in that designing) that students can use to evaluate themselves and each other for both the quality of the written speeches and the deliveries.

"Making Jokes on Paper"—Writing Humor

"Vonnegut is a postmodern Mark Twain," states Boon (2001), adding, "Continuing a trend in American literature that began with Benjamin Franklin, Vonnegut's style is ripe with irony and full of aphoristic wit" (p. x). Our English classrooms, as noted earlier, deal too rarely with nonfiction, and I would add that those same classrooms are far too often devoid of humor. Vonnegut offers wonderful humor for our students that fits well into an American literature tradition, which Boon acknowledges, and Vonnegut himself provides essays discussing his humor and how he constructs it. Klinkowitz (1998) explains that Vonnegut claims he and Twain "constructed [their writing] like jokes," similar to classic comedians such as Bob and Ray (p. 95).

To give students a richer understanding of how humor works and how Vonnegut uses humor throughout his writing, we can assign two of Vonnegut's essays from *Palm Sunday,* "Mark Twain" and "Funnier on Paper Than Most People." From these essays, we can help our students as readers and writers, expanding their grasp of written humor, irony, and exaggeration. Students, in particular, are more apt to react to and grasp physical and "gross" humor that they encounter in movies and TV, but more sophisticated satire—notably in text—

presents them with greater problems as readers because of their limited life experiences and limited experiences with humor in formal settings such as the classroom.

Speaking on the 100th anniversary of Mark Twain's house, Vonnegut talked in 1979 about his own view of Twain as "saying what Christ said in so many ways: that he could not help loving anyone in the midst of life" (p. 152). Vonnegut, like Twain, makes somewhat outlandish and at least disarming comments that are themselves humorous and insightful. These qualities challenge sophisticated readers; they also pose comprehension problems for high school and college students. Vonnegut offers readers a wonderful and brief introduction to Twain's skills as a satirist and a social commentator; as well, Vonnegut includes seemingly glib but valuable explanations about what makes any writing effective: "This is the secret to good storytelling: to lie, but to keep the arithmetic sound" (p. 153). The humor in Vonnegut's aphoristic style comes from the diction—"lie" and "arithmetic"—and the contrast between the weight of his topic and the breezy nature of his tone. Vonnegut, as with many humorists, dresses his serious subjects in a clown's outfit. In other words, Vonnegut holds both Twain and the craft of writing in the highest regard, but his diction and tone are light and even childish in spots. This tension created by a writer helps elicit laughter from readers, from audiences.

Beyond the stylistic qualities found in Twain, Vonnegut also discusses briefly the topics he shares with Twain—religion, technology, superstition, and the endless silliness of humans. While this section of *Palm Sunday* stands as an essay, it was originally a speech. But translated to print, readers see Vonnegut's comic timing in the paragraphing of the text:

> "'End quote.
>
> 'What a funny ending.'" (p. 155)

These one-line paragraphs, one of which is a fragment, are rich with sarcasm, following as they do a particularly dark passage from Twain's *A Connecticut Yankee in King Arthur's Court*.

By the end of this section, Vonnegut proclaims Twain as "the most enchanting American at the heart of each of his tales," like Vonnegut himself (p. 156). This comment by Vonnegut may establish Twain as a postmodern novelist and writer, but ultimately what matters to Vonnegut is the power of Twain's writing: "This is a miracle. There is a name for such miracles, which is myths" (p. 156). Great writers work within universal myths while simultaneously creating mythologies themselves; for writers such as Twain and Vonnegut, these modern and postmodern myths are ripe with irony, satire, and humor. This humorous speech by Vonnegut takes a decidedly sharp turn in tone at the end when Vonnegut admits naming his son Mark after Twain—again mixing a series of often blasphemous jokes with a clear statement that Vonnegut owes quite a great deal to the man he has been using as the source of his jokes.

ENTRY POINT

While I have discussed here that Vonnegut's "Mark Twain" is useful in our discussions of humor in our classrooms, the piece is clearly a perfect way to introduce students to many of the works of Mark Twain. Vonnegut mentions *A Connecticut Yankee in King Arthur's Court*, *The Adventures of Tom Sawyer*, *A Tramp Abroad*, *The Prince and the Pauper*, *Life on the Mississippi*, and *The Adventures of Huckleberry Finn*. As well, this essay could be an excellent entry point into many of Twain's humorous short stories.

With my high school students, I found that observing them as they watched Woody Allen's *Annie Hall* or Monty Python's *Holy Grail* revealed a great deal about their sensitivity to what we might call sophisticated humor. Some of their skill in perceiving subtle and ironic humor came from their life and literary experiences, while some invariably came from their innate cognitive skills. Regardless, students who are highly perceptive of humor at its most sophisticated levels are often our most gifted students with language. We need to expand on those students' abilities, and we must help weaker students develop a sense of humor *because* humor is a profoundly verbal thing. We can use Vonnegut's "Funnier on Paper Than Most People" as a vehicle for asking students the essential question: What makes humor humorous—especially in writing?

Many critics have equated Vonnegut's humor with stand-up comics (Boon, 2001; Klinkowitz, 1998), and Vonnegut himself has characterized his works as a series of purposeful jokes. "Funnier on Paper Than Most People" begins with bragging, setting the adolescent tone of Vonnegut's humor—"I am better than most people in my trade at making jokes on paper" (p. 157). This opening sentence shows the reader that the tone is established through the informal diction of "making jokes on paper." This essay was also originally a speech; by the second paragraph of the quoted speech, Vonnegut mentions "monkey business" along with the transcripts of college graduates. This incongruity of diction with the immediate importance of transcripts for college grads is a key example of Vonnegut's humorous technique as a writer and a spokesman. The speech includes early references to Kin Hubbard and Oscar Wilde; Vonnegut offers Hubbard and Wilde as different types of humorists, one more popular and one more literary. The commencement address quickly turns to Vonnegut's favorite skits—satirizing commencement speeches and discussing his favorite topics, such as extended families.

The overt purpose of the speech is to explain to the graduates and his readers why jokes work. Vonnegut's formula follows his favorite joke about cows making milk and cream. The formula includes:

> "How do jokes work? The beginning of each good one challenges you to think. . . .
>
> "The second part of the joke announces that nobody wants you to think, nobody wants to hear your wonderful answer. You are so relieved to at last meet somebody who doesn't demand that you be intelligent. You laugh for joy." (p. 160)

The formula itself is, of course, a joke. And Vonnegut is avoiding telling his audience the formula by showing us instead. The key element of a joke is the incongruity and misdirection that the writer or comic creates. In literature, humor is often drawn from irony in a variety of forms.

CONNECTIONS

Since our students will tend to have a greater sense of humor in movies, I recommend having discussions of how humor works using either Woody Allen's *Annie Hall* or *A Midsummer Night's Sex Comedy* along with Monty Python's *Holy Grail*. All three of these movies offer ample opportunities to discuss verbal humor, physical humor, and the differing levels of humor. Allen and Monty Python wander from sharp and intelligent humor to the silliest slapstick. A logical Vonnegut pairing with these movies would be his aptly named *Slapstick*, dedicated to the comics Laurel and Hardy. Students may benefit from viewing Laurel and Hardy movie clips or clips from the Three Stooges; these classic comedy teams are often unknown to contemporary students but can serve as accessible examples of types of humor.

Vonnegut tells us that he was fired (not so funny) from GE because he wrote a joke into a speech for a vice president of the company that left the VP unable to complete his speech. After his satiric formula for a good joke, he shares a silly poem, highlighting that outlandish or heavy rhyme makes a poem humorous—a sense all students have intuitively (from children's literature such as Dr. Seuss or Shel Silverstein) but often ignore when they attempt poetry themselves;

young writers will invariably use heavy rhyme in poems that are terribly serious, ruining their own effect because of their lack of awareness and purpose (unlike Vonnegut and other writers who are in control of their tone and intent).

Throughout this speech, Vonnegut writes as Benjamin Franklin did, depending on aphorism and comic timing that punctuate essentially serious themes. "I have several children—six, to be exact—too many children for an atheist, certainly" demonstrates his timing with the dashes and his pairing of incongruous ideas by mentioning his children (six children probably catches the audience off guard somewhat) along with making a socially uncomfortable confession in a rather offhand manner, that he is an atheist (p. 161). Humorists are adept at taking their audiences in drastically divergent directions as part of their purpose.

Another quality of humorists exhibited by Vonnegut in this speech is endearing himself to his audience. Here, he "pronounce[s] those about to graduate women and men" (p. 161). This is exactly what all young people want from adults, but this impromptu "puberty ceremony" (p. 161) also holds these graduates responsible for acting as adults (something they probably haven't considered fully) and lays the groundwork for Vonnegut to protest war—an abrupt twist to a speech about how jokes work. First, Vonnegut is funny and endearing; then he takes a difficult and often socially unpopular stance.

The speech approaches the value in reading and writing (and the difficulty in teaching reading and writing) along with the need for humans to have artificial extended families. Through this work, students can become more sensitive to writers' tools for humor and for using that humor for serious intent. Beyond simply reading Vonnegut to discuss humor, we can also reinforce students' understanding of broader techniques such as irony, paradox, satire, sarcasm, and parody. This piece as well can lead to asking students to write anything from jokes to humorous essays, assignments students are rarely asked to complete.

CONNECTION

One of the lingering struggles of the English curriculum at the high school and college levels is our need to address classic literature while also exposing our students to contemporary work. Vonnegut himself notes his indebtedness to the Greek playwright Aristophanes, who "wrote comedies that were . . . harsh indictments of the faults of Athenian society" (Marvin, 2002, p. 18). While dealing with Vonnegut's humor in his nonfiction, students may study a comedy by Aristophanes, focusing on social satire and how writers and dramatists create humor. Marvin also notes that Vonnegut was drawn to Aristophanes's "frank[ness] about sexuality and bodily functions, and Vonnegut brings a similar frankness to his novels" and his nonfiction works (p. 18).

- -

Considering and Reconsidering Reviews and Op-Ed Essays

Kurt Vonnegut the celebrated novelist has found himself at various times offering his unique style and rambling humor to book reviews and Op-Ed pieces—nonfiction forms that have been found in the traditional English classroom and should be revisited by teachers and students. "Everybody associated with a new dictionary ain't necessarily a new Samuel Johnson," Vonnegut (1968) ends his review—of *The Random House Dictionary* no less—with wit, controversy (he uses "ain't"!), and a literary reference that requires a certain level of sophistication from his reader despite the apparent anti-intellectualism running throughout the review. As Jerome Klinkowitz (Boon, 2001) explains, Vonnegut's nonfiction is notable for the "deliberate breaking [of] conventional rules," which allows teachers both to teach and to reconsider those conventions through his writing (p. 8). In this section, we will look at Vonnegut's book reviews and Op-Ed pieces for opportunities to ask students as readers and writers to explore and reconsider these forms.

Book reviews, dictionaries, prescriptive and descriptive stances—these are generally not the things we might associate with engaging activities for our students who might quickly roll their eyes at any of these. Yet, if we begin a consideration of book reviews with Vonnegut's review of *The Random House Dictionary,* we find that Vonnegut does breathe life into assignments and topics that have become stale and even dead over the years. This review by Vonnegut begins with, "I wonder now what Ernest Hemingway's dictionary looked like, since he got along so well with dinky words that everybody can spell and truly understand" (*Welcome to the Monkey House,* 1968, p. 118). This opening line sparks humor with "dinky" while also raising a very serious and ultimately interesting literary debate about Hemingway's reputed simplistic language and reputation as a major writer (himself a journalist like Vonnegut). The breezy tone and informal diction of this book review of a dictionary serves as an excellent example of Vonnegut's typical ironic approach to both his topic and his style. In the second paragraph, he calls the dictionary a "bomb," and then immediately qualifies his word choice by explaining that he does not mean the term negatively, but "I mean that the book is heavy and pregnant, and makes you think" (p. 188). His drastically shifting diction ("dinky" and "bomb" are woven together with "leviathan" and "pejorative") is combined with effective metaphor (that the book is "pregnant"), demonstrating for our students the craft found in a *book review*—a form they have probably discounted as simply something done for school (and not done very well, at that).

CONNECTION

Is Ernest Hemingway's prose filled "with dinky words that everybody can spell and truly understand"? An excellent pairing for having students explore diction and style is Vonnegut's dictionary book review and Hemingway's "Hills Like White Elephants." Vonnegut's review opens the door to discussing Hemingway's style and seemingly simplistic diction and sentence formation. As well, Vonnegut's pregnancy metaphor works in two odd ways with Hemingway's story. First, "Hills Like White Elephants" dramatizes a discussion between a man and woman who are facing a problematic pregnancy—and a veiled discussion of an abortion. Second, Hemingway's story, like all of literature, is itself pregnant with implication and subtlety.

"New Dictionary" can lead to a number of varied activities, assignments, and lessons; some of these include the following:

- Initially, "New Dictionary" can serve as the text for a discussion about student perceptions of book reviews (what they have been asked to do in English courses), about traditional book reviews found in newspapers and magazines, and about Vonnegut's manipulation of the form. A valuable assignment is asking students to write multiple book reviews about the same book, following different conventions or composing for different audiences.
- As a piece of nonfiction, "New Dictionary" can introduce students to a wider array of techniques used in creative nonfiction than students tend to consider. Vonnegut's humor and figurative language are but two elements of his nonfiction that are often missing in student writing—particularly for school assignments.
- For mature classes, Vonnegut's wandering into the inclusion of "dirty words" (p. 119) in unabridged dictionaries certainly will interest students and can lead to valuable discussions about the taboo nature of some words in some contexts. Vonnegut's noting the sexual meaning of "hump" in the review can lead to discussions of contextual meanings of words and about levels of diction along with appropriateness of diction for differing audiences.
- I have found that students engaged in authentic writing courses

eventually embrace and even enjoy discussions of Standard English when we admit that grammarians fall into two distinct camps: "To find out in a rush whether a dictionary is prescriptive or descriptive, you look up *ain't* and *like*" (p. 120). While I advocate a descriptive grammar stance in courses concerned with fostering writers (Thomas, 2005), I admit to students that there is a pervasive prescriptive attitude about language in our culture. For teachers, I recommend Constance Weaver's *Teaching Grammar in Context* and Joseph Williams's *Style* as valuable resources for considering this debate as well—particularly in terms of how that stance impacts the teaching of writing.

While it may be argued that Vonnegut wrote book reviews primarily as a way to earn money as a writer, it does not lessen the value of his book reviews for the classroom since Vonnegut demonstrates high-quality writing in these reviews along with practicing his skill as a humorist and a satirist. Also, book reviews tend to be relatively short, thus manageable for brief lessons in class. Most of his book reviews are woven into larger sections of his full-length books, such as *Wampeters, Foma & Granfalloons* and *Palm Sunday*. Particularly in *Palm Sunday*, students can benefit from Vonnegut reflecting on his reviews before and after he shares them, leading to other valuable and unpredictable discussions and assignments.

Let's look at just a few of his book reviews and how they might be used in our classes before discussing his Op-Ed pieces and his 2005 collection of nonfiction, *A Man without a Country*. "Oversexed in Indianapolis" and "A Political Disease" are included in *Wampeters, Foma & Granfalloons*, and his review of Joseph Heller is included in the "The People One Knows" section of *Palm Sunday*. Briefly, the discussion may include:

- Vonnegut's use of varying levels of diction and his adept manipulation of tone are central to his brief review of Dan Wakefield's *Going All the Way*, "Oversexed in Indianapolis." Since the review is short and a discussion of diction and tone would not require that students read Wakefield's book, this piece could be an excellent brief lesson. As is common with Vonnegut, the review also drops quick but sharp points about American culture, war, humor, and sex that may prove to be fertile ground for lengthier discussions.

- In February of 2005, Hunter S. Thompson, whose gonzo journalism made him a notable American celebrity and writer, died at 67; Vonnegut reviewed Thompson's *Fear and Loathing: On the Campaign Trail '72*, and this review can be used to introduce students to alternative approaches to journalism and the works of

New Journalists such as Thompson or as another model of book reviews. Vonnegut reveals his own political concerns within his discussion of Thompson's wild and raucous coverage of the 1972 presidential campaign. Further, the reader of this review has an opportunity to compare a campaign of more than 30 years ago with more recent campaigns.

- *Palm Sunday*'s inclusion of Vonnegut writing about the work of Joseph Heller shares some similarities with Vonnegut discussing Hunter S. Thompson in that Vonnegut seems to weave himself into his book reviews with the same power that he does in nearly all his writing, thus often writing as much about himself as his subject (especially when his subjects are writers with whom he has much in common). This review serves as an interesting model of nonfiction writing and of the review specifically because of Vonnegut's use of traditional and authoritarian statements (such as noting "Chekhovian techniques") that we might not expect in Vonnegut, his use of figurative language ("It is clear and hard-edged as a cut diamond"), and his much more developed content than in other reviews (p. 119).

A book review, of course, is an opinion, a specialized type, but much of Vonnegut's work ultimately may be called his opinion, though those opinions come in many forms. Throughout my teaching career of over twenty years, I have witnessed what most English teachers bemoan—the weakness of student writers when they are asked to write persuasion. Since this purpose for writing needs to be addressed in our classes, an authentic form of persuasion that students can encounter daily is the Op-Ed piece in our newspapers. Vonnegut includes a number of Op-Ed pieces in his full-length nonfiction collections and published in 2005 what could be considered a collection of Op-Ed essays, *A Man without a Country*.

The Op-Ed as a reading or writing assignment can work well in our classes for a number of reasons. First, the Op-Ed tends to be a concise form; most Op-Ed pieces I write have to stay within a 750-word limit. For students, requiring them to write an Op-Ed is essentially asking them to write a nonfiction prose-poem of sorts. Further, the Op-Ed is an authentic and vibrant form, unlike the traditional and stale assigning of a persuasive essay that results in students choosing lifeless topics and writing for no real audience other than the teacher. Syndicated columnists provide ample models as well of how Op-Ed essays are often driven by the persona of the columnist. If we bring a series of pieces by the same author to the class, possibly several by Vonnegut paired with several by a columnist who appears regularly in your local paper, we can have students analyze the techniques those writers employ to create their Op-Ed personality.

Two Op-Ed pieces included in *Palm Sunday* are brief and conversational, but they provide provocative statements about censorship in the first section titled "The First Amendment," and about the dangers of technology in "When I Lost My Innocence." His argument against censorship is an impassioned call to ban those who don't read from complaining about what books we place in students' hands. These pieces for *The New York Times* fit English classrooms perfectly as they are ripe opportunities for discussing with students what literature belongs in their hands—a discussion we far too rarely have with students themselves. Broadly, Vonnegut condemns those non-readers who gloat about not reading the books they attempt to ban: "But they have no business supervising the education of children in a free society" (p. 7). Particularly in the politically conservative climate of the past couple decades, Vonnegut's open praise of the ACLU may be an interesting focus for a discussion since some students will come from homes where the ACLU is held in a quite different light.

CONNECTIONS

In my American literature classes for years, students were required by the department to read Mark Twain's *The Adventures of Huckleberry Finn*. I often persuaded several students to read J. D. Salinger's *The Catcher in the Rye*. These two novels have maintained top spots virtually every year for decades as books most banned in America. I assigned persuasive essays to students dealing with why we should or should not require these books in U.S. classrooms. Justifications for assigning the books and arguments against requiring them both challenged students since the perspective of students has rarely been encouraged or honored. Further, students were often nearly oblivious to why adults often argued against these books. With *Huck Finn,* we have an interesting example of a book that is banned from a variety of political and cultural agendas. Some groups who are easily labeled from the Left have argued that the book's use of racial slurs makes it inappropriate for classes—although we tend to associate book banning with the political Right. Combining Vonnegut's Op-Ed and section in *Palm Sunday* addressing the First Amendment with often-challenged novels in the classroom helps students confront the complexity of the issue while also engaging them in authentic writing opportunities.

"But I learned how vile that religion of mine could be when the atomic bomb was dropped on Hiroshima," states Vonnegut concerning one of his most often addressed topics, technology—the "only religion of [his] family during the Great Depression" (p. 62). This open letter published in a Swedish newspaper details the contrast between Vonnegut's attitude toward technology during his youth and its change in his adulthood where he lived dramatically through WWII. This development probably matches well the naïve and somewhat blind trust that modern youth have in technology, a level of technology that far surpasses that of Vonnegut's youth. Modern students are perpetually attached to cell phones, laptop computers, and iPods; they may accept quickly Vonnegut's warning about the dangers of technology in large-scale tragedies such as war. What his essay may prompt is an opportunity to ask students to reflect in writing on the potential dangers of technology on much smaller and even personal levels. "It is supposed to be good to lose one's innocence," he offers in the letter (p. 63). We can use his argument to chip away at the naïve attitudes our students have toward the technology they not only take for granted but worship in ways not unlike Vonnegut's family who believed technology would save them from the poverty of the Great Depression.

CONNECTION

As the world drifted toward the newest millennium, Vonnegut published his last novel and proclaimed he would soon publish no more. However, he found himself increasingly popular as an essayist, publishing a number of essentially Op-Ed pieces in the alternative publication *In These Times*. His unique though left-of-center rants against the George W. Bush administration and general stupidities of American culture have been noted as the most popular parts of the magazine's web page, of all things. Collected as *A Man without a Country*, this surprise publication by Vonnegut is an excellent full-length look at one author making diverse and well-crafted arguments. Seasoned readers of Vonnegut love these essays but see little that is new. Students with less experience in reading Vonnegut may benefit from reading his perspective directed at the things of their immediate world.

New Journalism—Writing in Search of Truth

Some of the most authentic and valuable writing opportunities for students in our schools come in student publications when we are willing to turn over the responsibility for the newspaper and literary magazines to the students. Vonnegut himself writes often about his experiences writing on a daily high school newspaper staff and for college newspapers. For the past forty years or so, as well, American journalism has experienced two distinct and contradictory confrontations of what constitutes journalism. Vonnegut addresses the concept of New Journalism—associated with Tom Wolfe and Hunter S. Thompson—a redefining of journalism from the postmodern Left, and students are currently witnessing a right-wing attack on journalism manifested primarily in media, TV, radio, and the Internet. Vonnegut's own New Journalism should help students reconsider what the role of journalists is, how we conceive of objectivity, what the nature of truth is, and how we can and should distinguish among the many varieties of information found in popular media (from the news wars between CNN and Fox to the reality, or lack of, in reality TV).

"Thucydides is the first New Journalist I know anything about," Vonnegut proclaims in the Preface of *Wampeters, Foma & Granfalloons* (p. xvii). This unexpected association is followed by Vonnegut discussing the role of the journalist in his own reporting as a contrast to the traditional objective expectations for journalists: "Newspaper reporters and technical writers are trained to reveal almost nothing about themselves in their writings" (*Palm Sunday,* p. 68). For students, Vonnegut can be an opportunity to define traditional journalism and the post-alternative New Journalism; they can be asked to write a news account that attempts to be objective and one that puts them at the center, embracing subjectivity and personal viewpoints.

ENTRY POINT

An effective and engaging vehicle for addressing both satire and New Journalism is bringing clips from Comedy Central's mock newscast, *The Daily Show,* into the classroom. While virtually any episode of *The Daily Show* can be used to discuss the contrasts between traditional journalism and New Journalism, the web site Media Matters for America houses a segment from *The Daily Show* titled "The Secrets of New Journalism Success" (http://mediamatters.org/items/200503040002). The clip is both a satire of journalism and a wealth of information about journalism and New Journalism.

CONNECTIONS

"Biafra: A People Betrayed" and "In a Manner that Must Shame God Himself" can be paired with major works if we are looking for units that integrate various genres or full-length works. Writing that deals with Africa can follow students reading Vonnegut's work on Biafra, notably Chinua Achebe's *Things Fall Apart* (mentioned by Vonnegut in his essay), Barbara Kingsolver's *The*

Poisonwood Bible, and Alice Walker's *The Color Purple.* These works all deal with varying degrees of colonialism and the tensions between cultures when one dominant culture imposes its will on another. "In a Manner that Must Shame God Himself" leads naturally to Hunter S. Thompson's *Fear and Loathing: On the Campaign Trail '72,* which is reviewed by Vonnegut and included in *Wampeters, Foma & Granfalloons* (as noted earlier). Vonnegut's and Thompson's New Journalism may be a part of a larger unit dealing with the Nixon era.

Vonnegut begrudgingly sees himself as a New Journalist, but he argues that even New Journalism cannot go far enough. The highest form of truth is fiction: "And fiction is melody, and journalism, new or old, is noise," he concludes in the Preface (p. xviii). Students who are asked to explore journalism, New Journalism, and fiction will ultimately confront objectivity, truth, and the perspective of any writer or artist. Vonnegut's "Biafra: A People Betrayed" is an excellent essay and a solid piece for discussing journalism and New Journalism, along with "In a Manner that Must Shame God Himself," Vonnegut's coverage of the 1972 presidential campaign. Some of the lessons and assignments that can come from these two essays include:

- In contrast to the traditional teaching of the essay introduction, journalism has traditionally presented fairly strict guidelines for a lead in journalistic pieces. Both of these essays challenge how we view introductions and leads. The piece on Biafra begins in a fairly orthodox manner by discussing the Kingdom of Biafra and delays any use of "I" until well into the piece; yet, the campaign coverage begins immediately with Vonnegut musing about aliens visiting the U.S. in 1972. Both pieces can challenge students to reconsider how any writing can and should begin.

CONNECTIONS

While students are reading and writing nonfiction, particularly journalism, William Zinsser's *On Writing Well* provides valuable insight into how journalists and writers of nonfiction write engaging pieces. Zinsser's book is readable and accessible for students; as well, his discussions offer interesting and vivid examples from actual published pieces (unlike fabricated examples often found in textbooks). Zinsser's work is also notable for Zinsser's ability to be specific and clear without being artificially prescriptive. He is a successful writer discussing the art of writing authentically. After a few pages of discussing leads, in fact, Zinsser concludes, "Yet there can be no firm rules for how to write a lead," before offering the first line of the Bible as an example (p. 63).

- Both articles by Vonnegut feature Vonnegut himself prominently—a central characteristic that distinguishes New Journalism from traditional journalism. The use of "I" and the interjection of the journalist's opinions and perspectives are essential areas that students need to discuss in terms of the value (or even possibility) of objectivity. Vonnegut, like Hunter S. Thompson or Tom Wolfe, is an active participant in the events he is covering. In the contemporary world, debates about the role of journalists are increasing, notably centering on CBS anchor Dan Rather and the rise of cable news networks such as CNN and Fox.
- New Journalism also embraces a much broader range of tone than traditional journalism. Vonnegut's essays swing from many different levels of humor to both bitter and touching seriousness. In his Biafra piece, he promises to write about "the greatness rather than the pitifulness of the Biafran people," but laments at the end that he has "betrayed [his] promise" (p. 160). While he expresses a great deal of sadness concerning Biafra, he is much more biting and dark in his coverage of the 1972 campaign. Regardless of which piece students read, the work by Vonnegut allows us to discuss the appropriateness and range of tone in writing nonfiction.
- Paragraphing is often taught in English classes with the same sort of false dictums that poisons much of writing instruction. Vonnegut's third paragraph dealing with Biafra is, "Some tribe" (p. 141). Echoing his famous "So it goes," while also flying in the face of traditional requirements for paragraph length and even Standard English (Can "Some tribe" stand as a sentence?), this example is paralleled in "In a Manner That Must Shame God Himself," since Vonnegut is fond of one-sentence paragraphs that punctuate his sarcastic tone—"All the rest was hokum," he proclaims about the Republican convention (p. 189). Zinsser (2001) can again be a useful source for discussing paragraph as it applies to journalism and nonfiction (pp. 80–81).
- Journalism is often bound by time due to its references to people, events, and places that may have no meaning months or years later. Both of Vonnegut's essays are peppered with such references. This is a valuable discussion for students who are often taught the importance of universal themes in fiction and poetry. With Vonnegut's pieces, students can dissect how his many specific references both strengthen and weaken his work. Particularly with access to the Internet and a common search engine, students might enjoy searching for information on the many people noted by Vonnegut; this search could lead to a discussion about how background information about those people adds nuance and weight to Vonnegut's work.

Vonnegut's writings tend to blend and confront our perceptions of genre. His nonfiction admits that Vonnegut himself is at the center of that universe, while we suspect he is also at the center of his fictional universe. Vonnegut's nonfiction brings into the classroom many opportunities to force students to re-examine their assumptions and perceptions of the written word. As well, it forces us as teachers to do the same.

ENTRY POINTS AND CONNECTIONS

Timequake, Kurt Vonnegut

Walden, Henry David Thoreau

Black Water, Joyce Carol Oates

"My Speech to the Graduates," Woody Allen (*Side Effects*)

The Power of Myth, Joseph Campbell and Bill Moyers

"Teddy," J. D. Salinger (*Nine Stories*)

A Connecticut Yankee in King Arthur's Court, The Adventures of Tom Sawyer, A Tramp Abroad, The Prince and the Pauper, Life on the Mississippi, and *The Adventures of Huckleberry Finn,* Mark Twain

Annie Hall, Woody Allen, director

Holy Grail, Monty Python

Slapstick, Kurt Vonnegut

"Hills Like White Elephants," Ernest Hemingway

The Adventures of Huckleberry Finn, Mark Twain

The Catcher in the Rye, J. D. Salinger

The Daily Show (Comedy Central)

Things Fall Apart, Chinua Achebe

The Poisonwood Bible, Barbara Kingsolver

The Color Purple, Alice Walker

Fear and Loathing: On the Campaign Trail '72, Hunter S. Thompson

On Writing Well, William Zinsser

Chapter Three

Slaughterhouse-Five

Of Wars and America

"All of this happened, more or less," opens *Slaughterhouse-Five* in what avid readers would come to recognize as typical Vonnegut (1969) ambiguity delivered with a biting tone (p. 1). Vonnegut's career received a boost with the publication of this novel that would propel Vonnegut to the upper levels of both critical and popular success in a way that few authors ever experience: "Unlike the lure of many of his contemporaries, Vonnegut's appeal dissolves elitist intellectual boundaries. . . . [S]cholars and teachers have been increasingly drawn to his work, but so have lay readers, office managers, and computer programmers" (Boon, 2001, p. x).

As a permanently smitten fan and a dedicated teacher of Vonnegut, I have always wavered between wanting to share *Slaughterhouse-Five* with every student and feeling somewhat frustrated that most people know *only* this one novel by Vonnegut. What I have discovered, thankfully, is that Vonnegut's works tend to be infectious. When students are exposed to *Slaughterhouse-Five* and "Harrison Bergeron" in school, many if not all of them seek out more Vonnegut on their own. In some ways, for teachers, this novel is the safest avenue for introducing Vonnegut into the classroom since it has found its way into at least the modern canon of highly regarded works. While this novel has all of the elements of language and topics that draw the fire of those seeking to ban books, teachers can feel comfortable that a wealth of supporting material exists for the novel.

Since *Slaughterhouse-Five* is a widely assigned and taught work, I will deal with unique aspects of bringing the novel into classrooms in this chapter; I do not plan to explore the work exhaustively since it has a well-established presence—unlike some of the other works I cover in this book. Rosenblatt (1995) argues that "[l]iterature provides a *living through,* not simply *knowledge about*" (p. 38); with *Slaughterhouse-Five,* we certainly can offer students an opportunity to live vicariously through the firebombing of Dresden and the many horrors of war—as well as what it means to read a novel that defies the expectations many have for the genre. Vonnegut dissects the essence of America and confronts many of the Big Ideas that humans have wrestled with for centuries—free will, time, and human dignity. This novel also introduces students to the Vonnegut universe while offering traditional approaches to novel study and to teaching various lenses for literary analysis.

ENTRY POINT

In the opening chapter of *Slaughterhouse-Five,* Vonnegut confesses his struggle to write this story of the firebombing of Dresden during World War II. That explanation involves recounting his visit with war buddy Bernard V. O'Hare, whose wife Mary, "a trained nurse, a lovely thing for a woman to be," finally explodes in anger during Vonnegut's visit (p. 15). Vonnegut realizes that Mary "didn't want her babies or anybody else's babies killed in wars. And she thought wars were partly encouraged by books and movies" (pp. 18–19). This retelling allows Vonnegut to announce a moral purpose for writing the book, an antiwar novel, thus adding the subtitle, *The Children's Crusade.* Vonnegut's musing about the purpose of the novel can be a fertile area to ask students what the moral obligations of authors are. John Gardner's *On Moral Fiction* can be excerpted to ask this question before students read Chapter One of *Slaughterhouse-Five.* Gardner also argues against postmodern approaches to the novel, while endorsing the need for fiction to be essentially moral (he also directly discusses Vonnegut on page 87, prompting some interesting ideas about the quality of Vonnegut's fiction).

STUDENT INSIGHT

My ENG 11 students were both fascinated and puzzled by discussions of morality in fiction. While I found that my students had trouble defining "morality," I also discovered that they enjoy and even need to discuss the nature of morality, particularly as it is related to religion. Here are some journals by those students about the need for moral fiction:

> Writers should never compromise originality for morality. Progress implies change. We need writers to stray from the social norms that comprise the moral standard for a society. The most important thing that writers give us is new ideas and fresh stories. We need writers to be given freedom of speech so that they can cover all areas of life. Without the writer's freedom from the constraints of morality on paper, literature would remain relatively stagnant; restating the same ideas in the same way, again and again. It would forever be chained to one set of beliefs, and there would be no hope of gaining a new perspective on life. And without multiple perspectives, there can be no hope of coming close to understanding life.
>
> *Lee Neale*

> Writers educate. They want readers to be engaged in their entire work, whether or not the reader agrees. Writing certainly has the right to contain immoral events, acts, and language. Books that promote violence only create malicious thoughts. Mary O'Hare feared Vonnegut would portray war as a good thing for young men and thus trick young readers to join the war. This is a scary thought: Artists have the ability to create real life events, and then convince the reader to believe their point of view. Perverted artists convey immoral messages, which in turn destroys the integrity of their work. They can send hurtful messages. Yet the truth of the work, the bread and butter, must convey the writer's moral standpoint—or else their writing is false.
>
> *William Lucas*

> Writers have little obligation to be moral in the conservative sense. Freedom of speech and of the press defines their right to say whatever they wish. While what they say may be immoral, it is not their obligation to be moral. It is, however, the author's responsibility not to purposefully deceive the reader. This purposeful deception seems to occur more often in fiction than in non-fiction. An example of this is Dan Brown, author of The DaVinci Code and Angels and Demons. The DaVinci Code is a novel, but at the beginning of the work the author claims that everything contained inside is true. Obviously Dan Brown did not mean the storyline, so he was referring to the premise of his book and the acclaimed "facts" within it. Michael Crichton might as well have said that at the beginning of his Jurassic Park for all the evidence that supports Dan Brown's claim. It is worse, however, for an expert in a given field to purposefully deceive. These experts are using their position of superior knowledge about a field to manipulate not only their field, but more importantly, the public at large. Writing is done to convey a message, and when that message is twisted by a writer for the purpose of deception, the writer has violated his only moral obli-

gation as a writer. While freedom of speech and the press does still permit this, the writer has attempted to beguile his readers and hence should be vocally exposed to all of society as untrustworthy.

Chris Smith

Writers wield an amazing power to influence the mind of their readers. They control what their readers see, and the younger the reader, the more the writer controls what he or she thinks. It is their obligation to makes those thoughts moral for the reader. Writers always write with a purpose, and I would hold an immoral writer with the same esteem I have for cheating politicians and teachers who teach their students to lie, cheat, and steal.

Evelyn McKinney

Writers do not have an obligation to be moral. It would be nice if writers were moral, and only wrote what was morally acceptable to everyone, but how likely is that? In an ideal world, writers would be moral, but in our world, which is far from ideal, they don't have to be. What is the world without controversy?

Carly Roessler

"I have told my sons that they are not under any circumstances to take part in massacres," explains the narrator, "and that the news of massacres of enemies is not to fill them with satisfaction or glee" (p. 24). This pronouncement, apparently by the real Vonnegut, further establishes Vonnegut's intent in this anti-war novel. We will begin here with looking at *Slaughterhouse-Five* as a novel that is an anti-novel.

A Novel That Confronts the Novel

By the time our students reach high school and college English classes, they all have some level of assumptions about the conventions of the novel. Vonnegut as a writer and as a teacher of writing personifies a career that spans the rise of fiction writing that confronted those conventions throughout the mid- and late 1900s. This postmodern debate about what constitutes the novel—which is addressed at length in Gardner's *On Moral Fiction*—is both represented by *Slaughterhouse-Five* itself and confronted by Vonnegut as narrator in the opening pages of the first chapter: "As a trafficker in climaxes and thrills and characterization and wonderful dialogue and suspense and confrontations, I had outlined the Dresden story many times" (p. 6). For our students, reading and studying *Slaughterhouse-Five* can be an exercise in defining the traditional novel conventions while exposing the experimental qualities that many postmodern writers implement.

ENTRY POINT

Since students often respond well to video forms, beginning a discussion of conventions and experiments with those conventions with a movie is often an effective way to prepare students for similar lessons with the novel, a more time-intensive process. Woody Allen's *Love and Death* is a brilliant and funny parody of Russian literature and movies. The Woody Allen character speaks to the audience in much the same way that Vonnegut does in *Slaughterhouse-Five,* for example, making the movie an ideal entry point for the novel. Since Allen's movie also requires that the viewer have some knowledge of Russian literature, this opening activity can be an opportunity to teach students something about that literature along with discussing and reviewing the traditional characteristics of the novel. Further, both Allen's movie and Vonnegut's novel challenge students to consider the nature of humor and parody.

Students should begin by selecting a novel or novels that they have already read. From there, we can have them discuss the traditional characteristics we associate with novels and fiction—such as plot (and the linear pattern we often teach of exposition, complication(s), climax, and resolution), characterization, point of view and narration, dialogue, and the litany of literary techniques we teach through fiction. Much of what we address in our English classrooms falls within the parameters of the modernist period in American art and within the guidelines established by the New Critics of the mid-1900s. Depending on your aims as an English teacher, students can be exposed to these concepts as well, clarifying for them the expectations within the arts and within the critical fields.

The text and technique orientation of New Critical approaches to and expectations of fiction is the primary way we deal with novels in our classrooms (see Hedges, 1997, for a web-based explanation of New Criticism and a downloadable version of the outline). Directly and indirectly we tend to teach students to focus primarily on the text for meaning, uncovering the writer's techniques and calculating what meaning those techniques *added together* produce. These assumptions tend to ignore or devalue the life and perspectives of the writer and the reader along with devaluing the social context of the author during the writing of the novel and of the social context of the reader during the reading. While *Slaughterhouse-Five* certainly fits well into that traditional approach to fiction, Vonnegut confronts those assumptions as well, sometimes directly through his commentary during the narration.

Using the traditional characteristics of the novel, I will discuss briefly how we can include *Slaughterhouse-Five* in our classes both as a fairly traditional novel unit and a novel unit that challenges the novel as a form. While this novel holds a fairly secure spot in the canon of American literature, I will also discuss how and why Vonnegut's most celebrated work is or is not high quality literature. As the New Critic might, let's dissect *Slaughterhouse-Five* in order to make a fair diagnosis, as follows:

- *Characterization*—Traditionally, we announce to our students that the highest examples of quality fiction embody fully developed, round characters. Marvin (2002) notes that most "[c]ritics have frequently pointed out that Vonnegut does not create well-rounded characters" (p. 15). This might suggest that Vonnegut is a lesser writer, but Marvin notes that Vonnegut mainly writes satire, which thrives on more narrowly drawn characters. For our students, then, *Slaughterhouse-Five* can provide them with an opportunity to discuss and even argue the effectiveness of Vonnegut's characters, along with debating whether Vonnegut qualifies as a serious novelist. This novel has without argument contributed an unforgettable character, Billy Pilgrim, into the landscape of American literature, but are the characters in the novel of the same quality as those in *The Great Gatsby* or *The Adventures of Huckleberry Finn?* I mention these two novels since they are also driven by well-developed and vibrant narrators (a characteristic we will discuss next); I would add that Vonnegut's novel raises this question: Are Vonnegut's characters effective, or is his novel carried by Vonnegut's own voice, which permeates even the more traditional narration?

ENTRY POINT

"Several details in the novel suggest a connection between Billy Pilgrim and Jesus Christ," explains Marvin (2002, p. 124). Throughout English-language literature, we find Christ-figures, suggesting one way in which this novel does conform to some of the norms for literature. Students may need some introduction to identifying and explicating Christ-figures in literature. James Dickey's "The Lifeguard" suits this lesson perfectly. Throughout the poem, the lifeguard who fails at saving a drowning boy at a lake is portrayed with Christ and biblical imagery, both paralleling and contrasting the lifeguard's role as savior and failure as savior.

- *Narration and Point of View*—Students who have read even a few novels are sure to know that stories are told by a narrator (or narrators) and that point of view can be neatly identified as first person or one of two third-person points of view. More sophisticated readers know that these assumptions are far too narrow and somewhat misleading. In *Slaughterhouse-Five,* Marvin (2002) explains, the story "is a curious hybrid of fact and fiction that insists on its factual truth even as it uses fantastic fictional techniques," such as blending the narrator's role as somewhere between a third-person narrator and Vonnegut himself (p. 115). For students analyzing the novel, as with characterization, the issues of narrator and point of view become points of debate. We are forced to ask not only who is telling the story and how but also what impact those techniques have on the story and any messages in that story. In Chapter One, Vonnegut, the author, appears to be speaking to us, even telling us directly at the end of the chapter exactly how the next chapter begins and implying that the novel truly begins with Chapter Two.
- *Plot*—Narration usually follows both a neat chronological order and a fairly predictable pattern of development (noted above)—exposition, complication, climax, and resolution. Both Vonnegut's chaotic plot development and his thematic concern for time combine to present readers and students with a story that defies chronology, except for "presenting Billy's wartime experiences in chronological order, with one small exception at the end" (Marvin, 2002, p. 116). Billy Pilgrim appears to jump back and forth throughout the history of his life, and the novel introduces readers to aliens who perceive time in a dramatically different way from humans, Tralfamadorians. We might argue that Vonnegut's experimental approaches to plot, along with narration and point of view, are techniques that support a major theme of the novel, thus making his experimentation ironically traditional. Vonnegut recounts in Chapter One his own attempt at plotting the novel in a traditional way (pp. 6–7), but this story becomes something of a parody of plotting as he does the plotting with crayon on the back of a roll of wallpaper. This scene can be turned into an interesting activity for students, asking them to represent the novel's plot in some physical way, maybe with crayon on butcher paper.
- *Theme*—Students discover in their first days of school that books *mean* something; throughout school, students are universally asked what anything they read means. I deeply regret that we usually give the impression that any piece of literature is less important than what it means—although most writers themselves will argue just the opposite. I believe we can argue that Vonnegut offers

themes in his works as most traditional novels do, but that his themes themselves are what may catch readers off guard. Also, Vonnegut tends toward raising issues, instead of pronouncing neat answers: "Vonnegut explores . . . difficult questions and makes his readers think about them more deeply, without providing any definitive answers" (Marvin, 2002, p. 128). For high school and college students, Vonnegut may raise questions where many students have never gone before, causing them some discomfort and causing a few to revolt against Vonnegut and his work. When we bring Vonnegut into our classrooms, we must be prepared to discuss war, religion, sex, the meaning of life, the nature of time, Truth (and truth), and many of the assumptions of civilized humans and Americans.

If we put *Slaughterhouse-Five* in our students' hands, we might want to ask them, "What makes a novel, a novel?" From this essential question, students can refine both their understanding of the conventions of the traditional novel and the reactions against those conventions we find in postmodern and experimental novelists, such as Vonnegut.

Considering War—A Novel Unit

With social studies teacher and education professor Ed Welchel, I explored the need to address and the problems with addressing war through literature in our classrooms where students tend to reflect the socially reinforced patriotism of our country any time that we find ourselves at war (Thomas & Welchel, 2005). When we approach a novel unit on war, we must recognize the need to prepare our students for ideas and perspectives unfamiliar to them and uncommon in their lives, along with offering a great deal of background information regarding the historical context of the war or wars the novels explore. Vonnegut is not coy in *Slaughterhouse-Five*—both announcing the novel as an anti-war book and acknowledging the folly in attempting to nudge humanity toward peace and away from war:

> I said that [that he was working on a novel about Dresden] to Harrison Starr, the movie-maker, one time, and he raised his eyebrows and inquired, "Is it an anti-war book?"
>
> "Yes," I said. "I guess."
>
> "You know what I say to people when I hear they're writing anti-war books?"
>
> "No. What *do* you say, Harrison Starr?"
>
> "I say, 'Why don't you write an anti-*glacier* book instead?'" (p. 4)

Since art about and from war tends to speak against war, we might properly call this unit an anti-war unit, but nonetheless, this unit requires many elements in order to help students as they read and understand novels and to provide students with the appropriate support as they wrestle with some very difficult questions. The following discussion will describe a novel unit on war that includes *Slaughterhouse-Five; A Prayer for Owen Meany,* John Irving; *The Things They Carried,* Tim O'Brien; and *Catch-22,* Joseph Heller—two works dealing with World War II and two dealing with Vietnam.

ENTRY POINT

Both to introduce artistic responses to war and to prepare students for the nontraditional response to war found in art, I play REM's "Orange Crush." The song alludes to the Vietnam War, the reference to the soft drink evokes Agent Orange for the listener, and the lyrics are ambiguous enough and dependent enough on tone to challenge students who may wish to respond to war through their eyes instead of interpreting what the song is saying. The references in the song to "spine" and "collar" seem to suggest a highly critical attitude toward war. If students struggle with recognizing the anti-war message in the song, I highly recommend following up listening to the song with watching the stark and effective music video (available on DVD, *Pop Screen,* 1987).

A number of sources and opportunities are available, particularly through web-based activities, to have students gain the background and historical information they need to read and discuss novels about WWII and Vietnam, but along with this content information, students need some experiences with the ideas surrounding war and the wide range of opinions concerning war and peace. Either as an opening section of the novel unit on war or as separate assignments completed before this war unit, we can have students read and discuss Henry David Thoreau's "Civil Disobedience," Barbara Kingsolver's "And Our Flag Was Still There" (*Small Wonder*), and Chapter Five of Howard Zinn's *Declarations of Independence.* These nonfiction discussions of war are made even more effective by including as a unit or throughout the course a series of poems dealing with war; some I have used with a great deal of success are James Dickey's "The Performance" (WWII), William Stafford's "At the Un-National Monument Along the Canadian Border," Walt Whitman's "Beat! Beat! Drums!," Stephen Crane's "War Is Kind," Carl Sandburg's "Grass," Randall Jarrell's "The Death of the Ball Turret Gunner," and e. e. cummings' "'next to of course america i."

STUDENT INSIGHT

Students currently live in a relatively unique time of war—a war on terror, as we have come to call it. When reading *Slaughterhouse-Five,* they are confronted by a writer who experienced WWII and who feels compelled to speak against Vietnam, the war occurring when the book was written and published. My ENG 11 students were asked to ponder if war could be justified while they read Vonnegut addressing his distinct views about WWII and Vietnam:

> I believe wars can be justified as long as they meet certain criteria. I have always known to love my neighbor and to follow the golden rule, but sometimes war is necessary. The main issue surrounding war and major conflict is what we are fighting over. Many issues warrant special attention such as genocide, the murders of innocent people, and major oppression of people's inherent rights. Conflicts over different government ideologies (which may not harm the people), resources, and other non-danger issues should be avoided.
>
> Jonathan Andersen
>
> War is justifiable if it is supporting moral reasoning. World War II was a justified war, and I believe that the War on Terror is a justified war as well, but I won't touch on it too much since every person, no matter democrat, republican, or liberal, has a different opinion on the subject. Unjustified war is sacrificing people for personal benefits or for gaining territory or for gaining resources. The genocides in Africa are unjustified. It's like the REM song, kill what you don't understand.
>
> Joel Stiff
>
> Wars can be justified if they will save people. Wars for territory or over religious issues are not justified. To battle over religion is like battling over what will happen in 2080. There is no way to know the truth about what will happen. Therefore, there is no point in battling over it. Everybody knows that WWII was justified because Hitler had to be stopped. Hitler's threat was a reality and to delay even longer would have been even more disastrous. The war in Iraq is not justified. The basis for it was the possibility of Iraq having weapons of mass destruction. That was a possible threat, but not an actual threat because nobody knew if Iraq actually had the weapons. Wars can be justified, but often countries jump the gun and go to war before trying other possibilities.
>
> Kyle Beaulieu
>
> Wars are a fixture of human existence. History tells us that. It truly would be more effective to write a book against glaciers than one against war. It seems that war must be able to be justified, but then again, does any-

one really know what justice is? I can't put it into words. Socrates tried. However, everyone knows what justice looks like. If I had to interpret what Vonnegut thinks about justice and wars, (and I may be completely wrong) I would say something like this: The cause for wars is sometimes justifiable, but the actions of war are very seldom justifiable on an individual basis. I think wars may be one of those things in life that you just cant apply a standard formula to, and say "Yes, this is justifiable" or "No, it isn't."

Weston Dravenstadt

- -

I would begin this novel unit by briefly introducing the four novels and the writers; then I would either randomly assign students to individual novel groups (having each group be the expert group for one novel only and requiring each group to prepare a presentation on their novel for the whole class, possibly following up by asking all students to choose one more novel from the remaining three to read as an independent project) or allow students to rank which novel they would prefer to read and discuss, assigning them in balanced groups based upon those choices as best as possible. Another option, if we want to have all the students read Vonnegut, is to assign *Slaughterhouse-Five* to the entire class and place students in three groups focusing on each of the other novels. The assigning of these novels will prove to be less important than the lessons themselves.

- -

CONNECTIONS

Since the literature and films that deal with WWII are numerous, we might find opportunities to focus a single unit on WWII or ask a social studies teacher or history professor to offer a unit that pairs Elie Wiesel's *Night* with the movie *Schindler's List*. One of my most vivid memories concerning teaching English centers on this unit. I assigned *Night* to a class of ninth graders with very low literacy skills believing the book was both engaging and readable—a sure success! Early into reading aloud and discussing the book, I realized that they simply were not engaged. At that point I sent home letters gaining permission to show *Schindler's List*. The movie brought the reality of the Holocaust home for those students, who asked to return to *Night* after we viewed the movie.

- -

The four-novel unit I am suggesting here has some interesting and challenging dynamics that make the unit extremely fertile. Let's look at some of the ways in which this unit can be implemented in our classes:

- Since *Slaughterhouse-Five* and *Catch-22* deal with WWII and *A Prayer for Owen Meany* and *The Things They Carried* are about Vietnam, students can begin to distinguish how wars are similar and how these two wars differed, particularly in the reactions to them by the American public. Vonnegut writes in many of his works that WWII was a just war, but that Vietnam was not. Students could debate if this distinction is false or accurate; Zinn's works often help with this debate as well.
- Many students in high school and college are just beginning to recognize the political nature of life. These novels are rich with opportunities for exploring the political nature of novels along with the political aspects of war. From the role of political leaders in war to the role of political protests against war, these novels and the wars they explore allow students to discuss the complexities of politics at many levels.

CONNECTION

A manageable yet relatively complex dramatization of war and its impact on adolescents is John Knowles' *A Separate Peace*. This novel has Phineas, Gene, and their group of friends openly confront and discuss how older men send younger men to war. The political nature of war and of human interaction is at the center of this entire novel, from the boys struggling for academic superiority to the sporting events to their varying experiences with being caught in the machinery of war. Many students may have read this novel in earlier grades and could be asked to see it in a new light. This work is certainly also one that students could study independently.

- As noted above, these novels are separated by different wars; they are also distinct in their tones. Interestingly, the two WWII novels by Vonnegut and Heller share dark humor and satire, while Irving's and O'Brien's Vietnam works are essentially realistic and serious in tone (although Irving's novel includes surreal elements as well). Students can discuss how these varying tones affect how the reader sees the themes and topics, and they can also consider why the WWII works are more satirical than the Vietnam works.
- These war novels share qualities that are common to many war novels—they are primarily by white males and deal with a uniquely male world. Those characteristics can be used effectively in the classroom to consider the race, culture, and gender issues of the novels. While I support fully the need to diversify the canon of our classrooms according to race, culture, and gender, I also feel

that we can use works by authors who fit a traditional profile (white and male) to discuss how those works make assumptions about these qualities, how these works do address diversity, and how authors and people of differing backgrounds might address the same issues. Although Vonnegut is negatively criticized for the roles of women in this novel and other works, Irving's *Prayer* makes key and vivid points about the disproportionate impact the Vietnam War had on the poor and on African Americans. We might ask, for example, "Does Irving's race make his racial themes any less valid?"

- Vonnegut throughout his career has noted many times his belief that WWII was a just war—even though he espouses a pacifist stance—while Vietnam was an unjust war. In many ways, American society echoed that sentiment. While studying this war unit, students should have this debate while trying to unravel a stance on war and peace for themselves. Broadly, all four of these novels portray war as dehumanizing and horrific (and absurd) even when the reasons for the war and the results of the war appear to create more benefits for humanity than regrets and loss of life. Further, contemporary students should be asked to apply this discussion to the wars of their own lives, primarily the conflicts in the Middle East during the past twenty years.

Whether we bring *Slaughterhouse-Five* into our classrooms alone or as some part of a unit on war novels, we will probably face problems concerning the message and questions offered by Vonnegut as they contrast with our students' perspectives and their experiences with *debating* war and the subsequent issues related to the U.S. government. I believe using any lessons or literature to propagandize students can never be tolerated in American schools; however, I am aware through experience that introducing skeptical and liberal perspectives into essentially conservative settings (which most schools by their nature are), especially during periods of heightened concern for homeland security, creates a situation ripe for misunderstandings. For me, Vonnegut simply personifies the complexity of perspective since he offers nuanced stances and more questions than neat solutions.

Certainly, *Slaughterhouse-Five* and *A Prayer for Owen Meany* seem to call on their readers to reject war—or at least embrace war in only the most extreme circumstances. Ultimately, we as teachers and the authors themselves would settle for making some positive impact on students concerning their ability to be humane.

Dissecting the United States of America

Marvin (2002) explains, "*Slaughterhouse-Five* is a book about World War II, but it is also a book about America in the 1960s. It is both a product of its times and an astute commentary on them" (p. 133). I would add that the novel raises some key questions about the essential nature of America as well. Marvin and other critics have identified several core aspects of America that Vonnegut tends to challenge; our students should begin to consider such issues as well:

- Howard W. Campbell, Jr. (a character who appears in other Vonnegut works, centrally in *Mother Night*) speaks as an American who functions as a Nazi propagandist during WWII. Campbell's monograph proclaims: "*America is the wealthiest nation on Earth, but its people are mainly poor, and poor Americans are urged to hate themselves*" (italics in novel, p. 164). Marvin (2002) notes that Campbell makes a fairly damning claim about America's embracing Social Darwinism (p. 120). For students, the novel can be a platform for debating Social Darwinism as well as for considering whether Americans do embrace such a concept and should we. Regardless of how students stand on this narrow issue, Vonnegut asks his readers to look at the moral implications of who has wealth and who is impoverished in America—as well as why wealth is distributed as it is in this country. In late 2005, hurricanes Katrina and Rita and their impact on the Gulf coast raised America's concern for how the poor are unequally impacted, providing contemporary events for students to connect with Vonnegut's themes.
- Recurring throughout Vonnegut's works is his skepticism of consumerism and capitalism—two sacred elements of the American way. Marvin (2002) argues, "Billy's materially prosperous but spiritually empty life demonstrates that consumerism is no replacement for the fundamental values that many Americans abandoned after the war" (p. 133). Vonnegut's overt sympathy for socialism stands in stark contrast to the average American's unsophisticated understanding of socialism, communism, and Marxism along with Americans' blanket discounting of any system other than capitalism. For our students, this contrast can be very disconcerting. But discussions of the novel will lend themselves to these larger considerations of America. It may be painful, but students will benefit from reflecting on their own concepts of consumerism along with analyzing American expectations for a consumer-driven country.
- From WWII to Vietnam to the military actions in the Middle East over the past twenty years, Americans have been faced with the irony of taking innocent life during our proclaimed efforts to free

people living in oppressed circumstances. The specifics of Nazi, communist, or terrorist rule are unified by the American goal of bringing democracy and free-market economies to people suffering under totalitarian regimes. How have Americans in the past and how do Americans today (including our students) justify that contrast between taking innocent life and bringing freedom to people? *Slaughterhouse-Five* addresses that tension and even seems to distinguish between the tension during WWII and Vietnam, just as he makes such a qualification about U.S. military action in Iraq in his latest collection, *A Man without a Country*.

American dialogues and arguments have gravitated toward dichotomous claims such as "You are either with us or against us," reducing most public discussions to ideological rants. Students are more often than not exposed to the non-productive arguing that we hear on right-wing talk radio and TV; as a result, they have few skills or experiences with addressing big issues skeptically. In fact, many students believe to question is to reject. Vonnegut's novel can show that skeptical and complex dialogue is an essential aspect of a democracy—not a strategy to condemn and destroy our nation.

The Big Questions of Life—Free Will, Time, and Human Dignity

Challenging justifications for war and confronting the central elements of American ideology mean confronting Big Issues, but Vonnegut also tends to face other Big Issues that we can broadly call philosophical, such as whether humans have free will, what is the nature of time, and what responsibilities do humans have for the dignity of other humans. Students in high school and college are themselves often struggling with these and similar philosophical issues. If students find nothing else in *Slaughterhouse-Five* relevant, they surely will find some value in debating the philosophical questions raised throughout the work.

Vonnegut implements several techniques to raise philosophical questions. The alien race of Tralfamadorians force Billy Pilgrim and the reader to reconsider both free will and the nature of time. A Tralfamadorian states to Billy, "'Only on Earth is there any talk of free will'" (p. 109). For young readers, determining where Vonnegut stands on the issue of free will and deciding where he wishes his readers to stand can prove to be a challenge. Are we as readers to see the Tralfamadorians as adept critics of human frailties, or are we to reject the aliens as we embrace the fact of our free will? Marvin (2002) sees the Tralfamadorians as fatalistic and parallel to the Nazi mentality that "allow[ed] them to avoid assuming responsibility for their actions" (p. 118). I have found that students both enjoy and struggle with debating humanity's free will; I also believe that facing such challenging philosophical issues through literature provides students a relatively safe avenue for dealing with hard questions.

STUDENT INSIGHT

When I approached my ENG 11 students about free will, we discovered that they had trouble distinguishing between "freedom" and "free will"—a distinction that we addressed. Here are some considerations of free will by those students:

> In regard to free will, I'd say as sure as I am sitting here typing this response that I am a free person. I can move my arms and legs every which way; I might not be that flexible, but heck yeah, I am free. Now if I were to try and do a split, I most likely would suffer some painful consequences, but I certainly have the option of subjecting myself to them. The same principles apply with law if you really think about it. This is the part that government and law officials don't tell you: You are free to do whatever you please! Just like with the pain accompanying a split, breaking a law might not be the best idea, but your free will does not limit you. Enforcement of laws is only a deterrent from breaking them. Laws CAN be broken; nothing can control individuals in an absolute way.
>
> *[name withheld]*

> I'm not sure. Free will in the sense that we think we have free will? Sure. Whether or not this is the case or not, it's hard to tell. I believe that there is already a future that is GOING to happen, and it can be interpolated what it will be from current surroundings, but the fact that it is set in stone? No. It's hard to explain the position. Basically, it's guaranteed something will happen, and that thing that will happen is certain, but anything beyond that is pure speculation, to the point that even if we didn't have free will, we would never know it. A starting point, an endpoint, but no middle?
>
> *David White*

> Before I came to [college], I'd never really meditated on the concept of free will or worried about, but, after two terms here, apparently the subject mandates careful attention and merits debate. . . . After reading the Iliad and Exodus, my once positive outlook on free will was questioned and to some degree dismantled. How could the Greeks and Trojans have any control while the gods controlled every action and outcome? How could the king not reject Moses after God hardened his heart? These questions both puzzled and disheartened me because I began wondering if I had any truly significant input in my own life. I still have no firm stance on free will. I understand that humans under a government never have absolute free will, but

I would like to believe that I choose to subjugate myself to the government, not that a higher power unknowingly alters my ultimate end.

Brandon Craig

To me, predestination is the exact opposite of free will. The big question is, do humans really have free will or is it all predestination? I have had numerous conversations about this with people that I really respect spiritually, and being a Christian I felt like I should have an opinion and some way to back it up, and I believe I have come to a conclusion. Two verses in particular, Luke 19:10 and 2 Peter 3:9 have solidified my beliefs. . . . Those two verses lead me to believe that if God would allow us to choose our own eternal destination, heaven or hell, then he certainly allows us free will in our everyday lives. While God knows what we are going to choose to do, he still lets us decide for ourselves the choices we will make.

Jordan Sorrells

- -

The Tralfamadorian concept of time and Billy's time travel are additional techniques that challenge the reader to reconsider our linear understanding and assumptions of time. This issue moves beyond the argument over free will into a much more speculative and less resolvable debate about time, but Vonnegut's concern for time through art parallels scientific considerations of time, notably Einstein's writings and theories that straddle science and philosophy. Vonnegut returns throughout the novel to a "'bugs in amber'" image that forces the reader to contemplate the value in each moment of existence; juxtaposed with the chaotic narrative of the novel and Billy's own time travel, the frozen image of the bug also asks the reader to comprehend how past, present, and future interact on those frozen moments.

At the end of Chapter One, Vonnegut as narrator has an interesting take on Lot's wife: "But she *did* look back, and I love her for that, because it was so human" (p. 28). If any theme encompasses *Slaughterhouse-Five* and all of Vonnegut's work it may be his genuine affection for the potential within humans; combined with that affection is his call for all humans to be humane to each other. Vonnegut is a self-proclaimed atheist who embraces Jesus' call for people to love each other. Throughout the novel, many of the plot elements, techniques, and themes merge at a simple yet vivid point about the sanctity of the human spirit and a somewhat puzzling but apparent trust in humanity despite the overwhelmingly dark story and attitudes of many of Vonnegut's characters.

We can approach *Slaughterhouse-Five* in a traditional way, as an anti-war novel, and we can also see it as a provocative philosophical novel. Vonnegut remains Vonnegut with elements that suggest this is a science fiction novel or a work of satire. That Vonnegut's most celebrated work weaves so many approaches and concerns into a single novel helps convince me of his genius and of the value of bringing his work into our classrooms.

The Vonnegut Universe

Novels (and all reading assignments in English classes throughout modern history) have languished under the unwillingness of students to read. Often students do not want to read assigned works. Part of the explanation for this—one that I embrace fairly well—is that coercion itself dissuades many young people from reading. Another explanation is that we simply assign the wrong works—notably to male students. One quality that seems to stand out among students who like to read is the tendency to focus on one writer, one genre, or one serialized set of works. I first became hooked on reading when I discovered science fiction and then proceeded to consume everything written by Arthur C. Clarke.

I am convinced that this early obsession with genre and one writer was later paralleled by my similar mania for the novels of William Faulkner, whose literary works tend to remain within his fictional Mississippi county, Yaknapatawpha, populated by his unforgettable cast of characters who are woven throughout many of his works in varying degrees of importance. Vonnegut also creates his own fictional universe, his own band of characters who pop up in many works throughout his career. Such is the case with *Slaughterhouse-Five*, a novel that often serves as many readers' introduction to Vonnegut and his universe. Let's look briefly at the significant and recurring characters brought on stage by Vonnegut in this novel:

- Billy Pilgrim—The hero of the novel is, appropriately, the antihero of an anti-novel that is anti-war. Billy is one of the most memorable characters in modern literature despite his "passivity mak[ing] him an unlikely hero for a war novel" (Marvin, 2002, p. 124). Billy serves as a Jesus figure, as a commentary on modern America, and as a vehicle for Vonnegut's musings, but, despite what many readers assume, Billy is *not* Vonnegut. The character of Pilgrim "is based on an American prisoner, Edward Crone," known by Vonnegut during WWII (Marvin, p. 124).
- Tralfamadorians—The aliens of *Slaughterhouse-Five* have become part of the Vonnegut mystique. Even sophisticated readers struggle with how one should interpret the views of these aliens. Vonnegut appears to mix both ideas he supports and ideas he refutes into the Tralfamadorian view of the universe, leaving

these unique creations as primarily a technique for challenging the reader.
- Vonnegut—Yes, as with many of his works, Vonnegut himself seems to be both a persona within the work and simply the unadulterated voice of the man Kurt Vonnegut. Many critics and Vonnegut suggest that *Slaughterhouse-Five* is a characterless novel; it does appear to be true that the novel is populated with flat characters, and the story is driven by the narrative voice (Vonnegut or some persona of Vonnegut?).
- Eliot Rosewater—A minor character in *Slaughterhouse-Five*, Rosewater is the title character in Vonnegut's *God Bless You, Mr. Rosewater* (1965). Billy meets Rosewater in the VA hospital; there, Rosewater shares Kilgore Trout's writing with Billy.
- Kilgore Trout—Billy is not Vonnegut, but Trout appears to be Vonnegut's alter-ego of sorts, although even that may be an unfair pronouncement since Vonnegut himself maintains such a high profile in his own works. Trout is an unsuccessful science fiction writer, and he appears often in Vonnegut's works, most prominently in *Breakfast of Champions*. Marvin (2002) notes that "Trout allows Vonnegut to express his frustration with the publishing industry, critics, and the American reading public" (p. 126).
- Howard W. Campbell, Jr.—The central narrator of Vonnegut's *Mother Night* (1962), Campbell is an American serving as a propagandist for the Nazi's during WWII. As noted above, Campbell speaks from a morally suspect platform but appears to make insightful criticisms of America that Vonnegut supports.

CONNECTIONS

Obviously, we can match Vonnegut novels since he uses recurring characters. With *Slaughterhouse-Five*, then, we might pair *God Bless You, Mr. Rosewater, Breakfast of Champions,* or *Mother Night* in class or as out-of-class assignments. For students, a relevant assignment can be exploring what these recurring characters mean or represent for the reader and for Vonnegut, throughout his works. A challenge for most readers is ultimately determining Vonnegut's sympathy for these characters along with how we might feel about them. Within Vonnegut's universe, characters are not easily identified as good or bad, moral or immoral, sympathetic or repulsive.

The Vonnegut universe is a complex mix of futuristic science fiction and stark portrayals of the bleak life that humans have lived and do live in the modern world, the world since the invention and use of weapons of mass destruction. For teachers, I believe Vonnegut's catalog offers the best of both worlds—the allure of popular fiction and the quality found in serious literature. Bringing Vonnegut's *Slaughterhouse-Five* into the classroom can and often will lead to many students committing themselves to the Vonnegut universe, thus committing themselves to being avid and serious readers.

Traditional Concerns— The Canon and Kurt Vonnegut

If Vonnegut's *Slaughterhouse-Five* is both an experimental novel and a work that confronts controversial themes and beliefs, then what are we to do if our teaching circumstances prohibit assigning the novel for some reason? This novel can be, out of all Vonnegut's works, the most manageable to bring into the traditional canon and traditional classroom. While I am a strong advocate of expanding the canon— or even dismissing the concept of "the canon" entirely—I have lived through the tremendous challenge that exists for such an endeavor, despite how important it is to offer students works and ideas presented by a broad spectrum of writers, both male and female and among a diverse range of cultural and racial backgrounds.

Advocates of a fixed canon or a narrow definition of what works count as quality literature (science fiction is genre fiction, for example, not serious literature) rarely admit that *all* works now embraced in that narrow canon were, at some point in the past, outside the canon and had to gain access to "the" list. While I was researching the life of English educator Lou LaBrant for my dissertation, I had to smile often as I read LaBrant's own essays on fighting the fixed canon mentality; many of the works LaBrant noted as mainstays of the canon in the early 1900s were ones I have never read or taught! Teachers, their students, and the general public could benefit from gaining a richer understanding of how a work becomes recognized as quality literature. As teachers, if we wish to add *Slaughterhouse-Five,* a simple search of where and how often the novel is being assigned will establish for anyone the value in teaching the novel. This novel is often listed for the College Board's Advanced Placement course in Literature and Composition. Further, the novel is studied in many English courses throughout colleges and universities. If a teacher is concerned about others questioning her teaching *Slaughterhouse-Five,* I recommend that she first gather evidence that the novel is a mainstay of major testing organizations and taught by a wide range of college and university professors.

ENTRY POINT

Students usually have little or no awareness of the canon debate. In my classes, I introduced them to the debate on writers such as Emily Dickinson by sharing a chapter from traditionalist Harold Bloom's *The Western Canon* (1994). As teachers we can certainly benefit from reading through Bloom's narrow argument for what students should read; as well, our students should be exposed to the debate—how we decide what to assign in our literature classes and why people persist in arguing over those decisions. Vonnegut is uniquely well suited for this introduction because his work and his perspectives are somewhat ambiguous concerning traditional literature and postmodern literature, concerning the traditional list of "white male authors" and multicultural authors. The canon debate over how to decide what literature matters also leads to valuable discussions of why we read—and students rarely think beyond "Because our teachers make us."

While teaching high school English, I experienced one of the most surreal moments of my career when I was confronted by the high school librarian who was considering filing a complaint about my teaching Alice Walker's *The Color Purple* in my A. P. Literature and Composition course in which her daughter would enroll the following year. Yes. The librarian was considering censoring the use of a novel in an A. P. class. Her complaint stemmed from her doubts that Walker's novel is quality literature, her doubts that it belonged in the canon. The lesson I learned here is a valuable one. Showing her materials from the College Board and syllabi from colleges and universities had little impact on her concerns, but the point I was eventually able to make stood on my gathering for her and showing to her a large collection of critical works on the novel, critical works housed in her library. Vonnegut's *Slaughterhouse-Five* is supported by a wealth of critical analysis, notably Jerome Klinkowitz's (1990) Slaughterhouse-Five: *Reforming the novel and the world* from Twayne Publishers, a distinguished publisher for academic audiences (see Chapter One earlier for other critical works on Vonnegut and this novel).

An additional strategy for anticipating complaints about teaching Vonnegut's novel is to prepare lesson plans and assignments with the novel that are themselves not unlike plans and assignments with any novel. *Slaughterhouse-Five* fits well into traditional approaches to the novel and to literary analysis. That the novel satirizes traditional forms depends on Vonnegut working within those forms, ironically. Many students have focused on this novel and written excellent responses on the open-ended prompt of the A. P. Literature and Composition exam, many students have grown in their sophistica tion as readers and literary critics after studying this novel, and many students have become avid readers because of this novel. For those reasons, I have witnessed and I advocate the use of *Slaughterhouse-Five* in the most conservative and traditional settings without incident or disruption.

Expanding Critical Lenses for Students

As I have mentioned so far, students primarily approach literature with a New Criticism perspective, as we tend to accept this approach as "objective." While I argue that New Criticism is no more objective than any perspective, I do acknowledge that belief is dominant in the teaching of English. I also have discovered that preparing students as New Critics (they must know that this is how they will most often be asked to respond to literature) who have many critical lenses to choose from offers those students huge benefits as students, readers, and writers. Vonnegut's works are confrontational to perspectives in general, and students will find his works invigorating for their explorations as literary critics.

Since Vonnegut writes openly and often about his embracing socialism, his works lend themselves to Marxist criticism. Wading into socialism and Marxism proves to be a delicate thing in most classroom situations. Students have terribly narrow and negative impressions of the terms. Adding this perspective to their critical lenses will benefit them in more than literary ways as it forces them to have a more sophisticated view of capitalism, democracy, socialism, communism, and Marxism. Teachers and students will find a wealth of resources and information on Marxist criticism with a simple web search, but students can often begin developing a Marxist lens by considering these elements when analyzing literature:

- Marxist critics view literature as a reflection of the time and social structure within which it was written. The dominant forces of any time period impose their view of the world onto the society, and that dominant view often becomes the default "norm" of any society and in some fashion of that society's art (whether that art echoes that view or reacts against it). One element of Marxist criticism, then, is a concern for where power lies in any dynamic. In *Slaughterhouse-Five,* students might begin to analyze who decides the conducting of wars, for example. Vonnegut's novel clearly reveals assumptions about power concerning WWII-America and 1960s, Vietnam-era America.
- Marxist critics are also concerned about social stratification, the forces that create and maintain the class system in any society.

Vonnegut openly seems to criticize inherent flaws in capitalism for the creation of have's and have not's in the U.S. For our students, this debate and a skeptical approach to capitalism, the free market, and such will be something they have little if any experiences with. *Slaughterhouse-Five* (especially combined with *A Prayer for Owen Meany*) forces the reader to consider the American class system, but more intensely, it raises the issue of who fights American wars.

I do not pretend to be offering here an exhaustive discussion of Marxist criticism, or of any critical lens. But I do recommend that we all allow and encourage students to develop multiple critical lenses, particularly when they are confronted with works such as Vonnegut's. Just as Vonnegut's questions the status quo, students should use their time spent with Vonnegut's ideas to question themselves, including the traditional practices of the English classroom.

ENTRY POINTS AND CONNECTIONS

On Moral Fiction, John Gardner

Love and Death, Woody Allen, director/writer

"The Lifeguard," James Dickey

"Orange Crush," REM, *Green* (1988)

Night, Elie Wiesel

Schindler's List, Steven Spielberg, director

God Bless You, Mr. Rosewater, Breakfast of Champions, Mother Night, Kurt Vonnegut

The Western Canon, Harold Bloom

Chapter Four

Cat's Cradle

The Religion of Disbelief

"In *Cat's Cradle,* Vonnegut creates a new religion with a full set of scriptures and rituals, and he shows how it brings sense of meaning and purpose to the lives of people who have found no consolation in other religions," explains Marvin (2002, pp. 77–78). I would add that Vonnegut does this and much more—and that the novel forces the reader to wrestle with when Vonnegut is making a sincere point and when Vonnegut is being his most acrid and satirical; even skilled readers will struggle making that distinction. For me, this is one of Vonnegut's best novels as it pulls many of his themes together in a work primarily confronting religion.

At the heart of navigating this novel, teachers, students, and readers must come to grips with the fully formed religion at the center of *Cat's Cradle,* Bokononism. The novel begins with the narrator John requesting that he be called Jonah as he reveals to the reader that his quest to write about Dr. Felix Hoenikker—the scientist who is called a co-creator of the atomic bomb and sole creator of ice nine, the seed that causes the apocalyptic end of the world in the novel—eventually becomes his own journey to the Republic of San Lorenzo, where he converts to this new religion. Bokononism has its own messiah, its own text, and its own terminology that often parallels and parodies Christianity. Briefly, here are some of the essential details and terms:

- Bokononism is founded in part by Bokonon, born in 1891 as Lionel Boyd Johnson—"a Negro, born an Episcopalian and a British subject on the island of Tobago" (p. 103).

- Bokononism is outlawed in San Lorenzo as part of a plot by its founders, Bokonon and Earl McCabe—Bokonon "asked McCabe to outlaw him and his religion, too, in order to give the religious life of the people more zest, more tang" (p. 173). A poem captures this well:

  So I said good-bye to government,
  And I gave my reason:
  That a really good religion
  Is a form of treason. (p. 173)

- A *karass* is a team of humans that "do[es] God's Will without ever discovering what they are doing" (p. 2).
- A *kan-kan* is "the instrument" or avenue by which a person fits into his or her *karass*.
- One's *sinookas* are "the tendrils of [one's] life," those things and events of one's life that reaches out and mixes with other people's lives (p. 6).
- "A *wampeter* is the pivot of a *karass*" (p. 52). The nature of the *wampeter* is not that significant, although "[a]t any given time a *karass* actually has two *wampeters*—one waxing in importance, one waning" (p. 52).
- A *vin-dit* is coming to accept Bokononism and the acceptance of one's cosmic fate, "that God Almighty had some pretty elaborate plans" for everyone (p. 69).
- A *duprass* "is a *karass* composed of only two persons" (p. 86). That pair "always die within a week of each other" (p. 88). This may be what many of us call soul-mates.

ENTRY POINT

Both the concept of the soul-mate and the occasional news story of couples dying naturally within hours or days of each other intrigue students during their years when the pursuit of a mate becomes somewhat central in their lives. "The Luckiest," a song by Ben Folds from his *Rockin' the Suburbs*, has a speaker trying to explain his love to his soul-mate, we might assume. In the song, the speaker tries to express the depth of that love by mentioning a couple that would qualify as a *duprass*, since one passes away soon after the other.

- A *granfalloon* is a "false *karass*," and its meaning is captured well in a Bokononian verse:

  If you wish to study a *granfalloon*,
  Just remove the skin of a toy balloon. (pp. 91, 92)

- "The foot ceremony" that expresses universal love is *boko-maru,* "or the mingling of awarenesses" (p. 158).
- *Zah-mah-ki-bo,* in simple terms, is "Fate-inevitable destiny" (p. 184).
- "*Foma* are harmless untruths, intended to comfort simple souls," explains Vonnegut (1974, p. xiii).
- "*Duffle* . . . is the destiny of thousands upon thousands of persons when placed in the hands of a *stuppa*" (p. 199).
- "A *stuppa* is a fogbound child" (p. 199).
- *Pabu* is the moon, and *Borasisi* is the sun.
- To *saroon* is to "[acquiesce] to the seeming demands of [one's] *vin-dit,*" or fate (p. 202).
- Briefly, John fails his relationship with Mona because he is a *sin-wat,* "[a] man who wants all of somebody's love" (p. 208).
- *Pool-pah* is the "wrath of God" or "shit storm" (p. 244).

The quandary for readers in general and students specifically is how we are to respond to Vonnegut's religious concoction—Is it pure parody or a somewhat serious alternative to the failures of most religions? While Bokononism appears to be a revision of Christianity in humanistic terms—only humans are sacred in Bokononism—we must be suspicious of how seriously Vonnegut wishes his readers to view anything he creates. As I will discuss in the next section, *Cat's Cradle* appears ultimately to be concerned with raising some deep and difficult questions about religion, science, and art. And readers, students, and teachers are invited to consider these questions thoroughly though I doubt that any of us should find simple or easy answers.

Of Religion, Science, and Art

Readers and critics alike are often tempted to define Vonnegut's work narrowly, and I would suggest that temptation grows from his tendency to return to favorite themes and plots throughout many works—a concern for science and technology along with many novels that deal with dystopian or apocalyptic futures. These recurring characteristics of Vonnegut's work do fit neatly into a science fiction tradition, but Vonnegut appears to use these conventions with literary and thematic intent; as well, when Vonnegut returns to these themes and plots, he offers readers ever-changing approaches to them as he grows and evolves as a person and a writer. The worlds he creates in *Player Piano, Galapagos,* and *Cat's Cradle* are distinct, and as I will discuss, Vonnegut uses many nuances to the debates about science and religion, for example, to demand that his readers avoid oversimplifying the most complex issues that do face and have faced humanity throughout history.

CONNECTION

"What we have today is a demythologized world," proclaims Joseph Campbell (1988) in his *The Power of Myth* (p. 9). In this interview moderated by Bill Moyers for PBS, Campbell weaves together a wealth of his insight and knowledge about mythology and world religions; he also explores his own fascination with the power of movies to fulfill the human need for myth, notably in *Star Wars*. Campbell's own mixing of science and religion can serve as a strong and effective companion to Vonnegut's *Cat's Cradle*. For many years, I required the Campbell book for summer reading in my Advanced Placement Literature and Composition course since it provided two elements needed by my students—content knowledge about mythic patterns and religions, and an opportunity to explore ideas and concepts beyond their narrow perceptions of the world. A question raised by both Campbell and Vonnegut is, "How do science and religion address basic human needs?" Another benefit of pairing these works is that Campbell tends toward a positive discussion of science and religion, while Vonnegut is often likely to highlight how science and religion fail us—or how we fail them.

Marvin (2002) argues that Vonnegut creates an apocalyptic "vision of the world locked up in ice that will not melt," during an age when most people still directly feared a nuclear holocaust (p. 77). Written in 127 minute chapters, *Cat's Cradle* begins somewhat ambiguously by mentioning war, science, and religion within the first section. The first few chapters initiate the reader in the Bokononian religion that will grow in importance throughout the novel, but many of the early chapters are dominated by the narrator's failure to write another book (another repeated device in Vonnegut, the fictional book that grows out of the failed original book) about "Dr. Felix Hoenikker, one of the so-called 'Fathers' of the first atomic bomb" (p. 6). The life, death, and family of Dr. Hoenikker prove to be pivotal to the novel, and the doctor's own string game, cat's cradle, serves as the title of the novel as well as a motif that runs through the work.

Ultimately, *Cat's Cradle* becomes a book about religion that also explores science and art. Even though amoral science brings the end of the world in the form of ice-nine, a scientific catastrophe, scientists throughout the novel are portrayed as morally flawed, not scientifically flawed. One of Dr. Hoenikker's sons, Newt, shares a story about his father with John, the narrator. The story included in Chapter Six portrays a scientist without a moral compass:

> "After the thing went off, after it was a sure thing that America could wipe out a city with just one bomb, a scientist turned to Father and

said, 'Science has now known sin.' And do you know what Father said? He said, 'What is sin?'" (p. 17)

The apocalypse of *Cat's Cradle,* as noted by Marvin (2002), offers a contrast to the fiery end of the world fresh in the American psyche since the dropping of the atomic bomb during WWII. Ice-nine paralyzes the world with ice and comes out of the blue, as a Vonnegut character might say. For students, the novel seems to be asking, however, whether this is the failure of science or of religion.

ENTRY POINTS

Students today have a wide range of perceptions about and understandings of statements such as "the end of the world." Many students have read the Left Behind series by Tim LaHaye and Jerry Jenkins that explores a fundamentalist view of the end days, portrayed as a prophesy of the book of Revelation. Some students may be aware of the intense concern for nuclear destruction that permeated modern life from WWII until at least the early 1980s, when some believe the Cold War ended, but fewer students today have such a concept of nuclear holocaust. Before reading *Cat's Cradle,* two briefs works are suitable for opening the door to the topic of the world's end—Grace Paley's "Anxiety" and Robert Frost's "Fire and Ice." Paley's brief story dramatizes the modern anxiety over the possibility of nuclear war, and Frost offers a light verse about the argument over the end of the world—the scientific expectations of an ice age versus the religious apocalypse (which is paralleled by modern concerns over nuclear bombs). A light entry point into these two works is REM's song, "It's the End of the World as We Know It (And I Feel Fine)," which is actually not about the end of the world at all but a fun way to start students talking about the subject.

Cat's Cradle builds a complex web of characters and events that forces the reader to look carefully at those issues humans need to address, issues of existence and purpose, issues of truth, falsehood, and beauty. What, then, Vonnegut seems to ask, fulfills those needs best—science, religion, or art? The dominant theme that appears to encompass all of the themes of the novel is "the dynamic relationship between truth and falsehood that the novel explores" (Marvin, 2002, pp. 87–88). How well do science, religion, and art address truth and falsehood? We need to ask this question. Vonnegut seems to ask the reader to view these three areas in the following ways:
- Religion is highlighted in the novel through the new religion Bokononism. This concoction by Vonnegut has many parallels with Christianity, although those parallels seem to be parodies. Further,

Bokononism's philosophy expresses many humanistic concepts, or what Vonnegut would call Free Thought. Since Bokononism is part parody and part Vonnegut's ideology, that confronts the reader with a true dilemma. Students can be asked to analyze Vonnegut's many commentaries on organized religion, as well as the nature of truth and falsehood throughout the novel. Does Vonnegut make commentaries on Christianity or organized religion in general? Further, we should ask students to begin discussing and writing about their own perceptions of religion—its strengths and weaknesses.

CONNECTIONS

Vonnegut openly announces and explains his humanist and Free Thought moral structure in many of his nonfiction pieces. Both "Thoughts of a Free Thinker" (*Palm Sunday*, section 11) and "Do You Know What a Humanist Is?" (Chapter Eight of *A Man Without a Country*) are suitable as connections with religion discussions stemming from *Cat's Cradle*. This speech and essay help students define or redefine terms that are often misrepresented in general popular discourse, particularly in conservative eras such as the last couple decades of the twentieth century. "We humanists try to behave as decently, as fairly, and as honorably as we can without any expectation of rewards or punishments in an afterlife," Vonnegut (2005) offers (p. 79).

- Most, if not all, of Vonnegut's works shine a bright light on science and scientists. Other works by Vonnegut deal with science and technology more directly, but *Cat's Cradle* makes the sharpest cuts into issues of morality within science and for scientists. *Cat's Cradle* warns readers about the dangers of science and technology; ice-nine brings about the end of the world as we know it. This is nothing new in Vonnegut. Yet, throughout the novel, science and the role of scientists are dramatized as acts of assumed objectivity or amorality that are, in reality, acts of profound moral consequence. As noted above, the central scientific figure, Dr. Hoenikker, is portrayed as essentially naïve (as a child) about sin. Further, scientists state in the novel that humanity's trust in superstition instead of science is the essential flaw in society (p. 24). The average people of the novel, however, accuse the scientists of thinking too much (p. 33). These tensions between scientists and laypersons along with the tension between science and superstition (or faith) form the primary conflict of the novel that leads to the difficult thematic conclusions readers can draw.

Eventually science is defined first as the opposite of magic (p. 36), then as "the strongest thing there is" (p. 146), and finally as "magic that *works*" (p. 218). As with the topic of religion, science themes force the reader to consider the nature of truth and falsehood. A purer argument for students to debate can grow from pages 40–41 in the novel when characters raise a concern about the average person's understanding of the term "science" and of the nature of research. A profound disconnect exists over these issues in America and has serious consequences for both the field of science broadly and education more specifically (Thomas, 2004).

- A third concern of Vonnegut on a less-developed level is the role of art: "Joy and childlike wonder are also essential to the creation of art, and the role that art can play in the search for meaning in human life is another important theme of the novel," Marvin (2002) explains (p. 89). Science, religion, and art all share the quest for making meaning of human existence—although the avenues to those understandings are distinctly different. Marvin explains that Newt's painting and the architecture of "Frank's fantastic house" are "example[s] of how art can give meaning to human life" (pp. 89–90). Ironically, Marvin notes that architecture is something of a hybrid of art and science. Many artists use their art as a vehicle for endorsing the power of art; here, Vonnegut has challenged the intent and results of science and religion on a grand scale while infusing the novel with small tributes to the power of art. I might argue that he offers these three elements in a proportion equal to society's concerns for them. Art has a small role in the novel as it does in the real world. Further, the critical responses to Newt's art are cruel and negative (another Vonnegut stab at critics). Students may enjoy struggling with the value of art in society, particularly distinguishing between aesthetic value and utilitarian value (Newt's paintings versus architecture).

The novel ends with the final words of Bokonon, who begins the end of his scriptures with, "If I were a younger man, I would write a history of human stupidity," and we might assume that has been Vonnegut's quest all along. With the big issues such as religion, science, and art, humans fail far more often than we succeed. Students should be asked if this is an inevitable part of human nature or something that art can help us overcome.

The Importance of Names and Words

A recurring lesson of our English classes is the importance of words; more narrowly, we often explore with students the importance of names. In *Cat's Cradle* names of characters and the words unique to Bokononism carry both direct and suggestive value for the readers. As just one example of a larger issue, I use the importance of names in my classes to help students see the purposeful nature of writing *as a craft*. Many writers of fiction spend huge amounts of time and energy choosing names for their characters that infuse those characters with meaning. Students often find this fascinating; in fact, the most popular book in my classroom has been a book of children's names for future parents.

Marvin (2002) notes that Dr. Hoenikker's first name is Felix, meaning "happy" (p. 84). Marvin also discusses the importance Mona's name, echoing Mona Lisa. Once we show students that the names of characters matter, they are often eager to delve further into the work for these subtle messages. Beyond the meaning of names, however, I would add that this novel has character names that carry aesthetic weight. Newt, Hoenikker, Krebbs, Bokonon, McCabe—these are all harsh names. Vonnegut has created this cast of characters with purpose. We can also prod students to consider Julian Castle. Does the last name suggest anything? Is it significant that his initials are J. C., suggesting Jesus Christ?

Ultimately, raising the possibility of the significance of names in the novel accomplishes a number of goals. It gives students a strategy for attacking the text. As well, it helps them connect writer technique with textual meaning. On the broadest scale, it emphasizes the importance of individual words, and it helps students see the value in their own choices of words when they speak or write.

That emphasis on the value of words is also present in the wealth of terminology readers are forced to learn related to Bokononism. This aspect of the novel is extremely important for the classroom since it addresses the significance of words outside of our common language. Vonnegut's universe now includes some of the terms, such as "foma," "wampeter," and "granfalloon" (terms that serve to title one of Vonnegut's nonfiction collections). Some guiding questions are effective for asking students about this terminology:

- How do the terms of Bokononism impact the reader's understanding? Do the concocted terms impact how the reader responds to and understands the larger concepts beyond the terminology?
- Do any of the terms have some similarity to words already familiar to the reader? Do those familiar words impact the reader's understanding of the term?
- Do the terms or the concepts behind the terms have any solid parallels with mainstream religions?
- Vonnegut as the writer of the novel and ultimately the creator of

Bokononism had the pleasure of choosing these terms. What names would you give the ideas, events, and beliefs of your life that matter most to you? Why do you choose those terms?

Words and names carry many types of meaning—literal definitions and a series of connotations that often are unique to each person. Even the sounds of words and names matter to us. For students, approaching names and unique terms in a novel, again, gives them a strategy for uncovering meaning. *Cat's Cradle* offers a wealth of interesting character names and a unique vocabulary, both of which are central to the many themes of the work.

Parents, Children, and the Family

When I attempt to offer students some essential expectations for literature, I often suggest that many works of literature address in some way the tensions and conflicts that grow from family. Most critical discussions of Vonnegut note his concern for the role of the father in his works; as well, many of his works deal centrally with relationships among family members. Vonnegut's own deep affection for his siblings, his extended family consisting of birth children and adopted children, his two marriages, and his many references in his works to virtually every member of his family—all of these qualities suggest that for Vonnegut the family dynamic is artistically significant. In *Cat's Cradle,* family and the impact of family are key thematic elements.

Vonnegut's exploration of family dynamics grows primarily from the Hoenikker family. Dr. Felix Hoenikker serves both as a quest by the narrator and as an ever-present influence over the lives of his three children—Angela, Newt, and Frank. In a "Non Sequitur" comic strip (http://www.ucomics.com/nonsequitur/index.phtml), a man stands at the door of a Family Diner; the restaurant's billboard announces:

> **REAL** FAMILY STYLE DINING!
> TODAY'S SPECIAL: GUILT.
> (October 13, 2005, Wiley Miller)

Even comic strips seem to highlight the negative impact of family on us all. Marvin (2002) explains that "Dr. Hoenikker's three children all suffer from his failure as a father. Each one has a physical disability that is only the outward sign of a more significant psychic wound" (p. 85). Dr. Hoenikker and his children all seem to suffer the consequences of arrested development, but their childlike qualities challenge the reader to consider both the benefits and disadvantages of retaining childlike qualities into adulthood.

CONNECTIONS

The presence or absence of a father can greatly impact the dynamics of a family and the lives of each member of that family. American drama is rich with plays that illustrate this theme. Arthur Miller's *The Death of a Salesman,* Lorraine Hansberry's *A Raisin in the Sun,* and Tennessee Williams's *The Glass Menagerie* are all excellent connections with the family themes in Vonnegut's novel. Miller's play shows the force of a present father and the influence his corrupted dream has on his two sons while Hansberry's and Williams's plays dramatize the family living in the shadow of an absent father. These plays are also available in high-quality video versions that lend themselves to being shown in two or three class periods. Students focusing on family in *Cat's Cradle* could view any of these plays to offer parallel and contrasting views of family dynamics in literature.

At the center of the family theme in the novel is Dr. Hoenikker. His character is dead when the novel begins, having passed away on Christmas Eve. Dr. Hoenikker is a man who often plays with string—hence the cat's cradle motif—and who received a Nobel Prize. He is also a man who once leaves his wife a tip after she clears the breakfast dishes. Vonnegut appears to characterize his childlike wonderment as a strength of his scientific genius while also suggesting that his childishness manifests itself in a negligence of his family and his complete lack or moral grounding. Dr. Hoenikker is idealistic and driven, but he inadvertently scars his entire family and produces ice-nine, thus the end of the world. The ambiguous characterization of Dr. Hoenikker is paralleled by the ambiguous thematic messages associated with his character. Dr. Hoenikker is connected with Christmas and Christian symbolism throughout, along with being referred to as a "saint." Readers must negotiate what Vonnegut is suggesting with Dr. Hoenikker as a Christ figure, particularly when an elevator operator states about Hoenikker's death: "I said, 'Dr. Hoenikker—he ain't dead'" (p. 60).

While Dr. Hoenikker's character is ambiguous, the negative impact he has on his children is clear: "None of them has the emotional maturity to resist the temptation to use ice-nine to buy a little love and acceptance" (Marvin, 2002, p. 85). Just as Tom relinquishes his role as son and his Self to become the replacement father in *The Glass Menagerie,* Angela assumes the role of Mother for Newt, Frank, and her father when her mother dies giving birth to Newt. In Chapter Six, Newt describes this transformation of his sister and notes that "'Father was all she had. She didn't have any boyfriends'" (p. 16). As Marvin notes, Angela has physical characteristics that parallel her psychological problems; she is described as "the horse-faced platinum blond I had noticed earlier" (p. 111) by John, and she stands noticeably tall, in contrast with Newt's being a midget, "hunch[ing] over in a desperate attempt to minimize her height" (Marvin, p. 85). Readers might begin to wonder if Angela has no ability to be herself since she has lived her life as a surrogate mother for her dysfunctional family—the stooping over to deny her height, the bleached hair.

"About this Frank Hoenikker—the pinch-faced child spoke with the timbre and conviction of a kazoo," explains John about the 26-year-old general on San Lorenzo (p. 194). Frank spends much of his life from childhood until San Lorenzo seeking "power over living things" and "play[ing] God on a small scale, just as his father is playing God by creating weapons that can destroy life on earth" (Marvin, 2002, p. 86). Again like his father, Frank appears to have no moral compass; he spends his life after the apocalypse of ice-nine ruling over his collection of ants: "The ants could do nothing without Frank's catching them at it and commenting upon it" (p. 280). Frank contributes to the theme in the novel through his house—"The effect of the house was not so much to enclose as to announce that a man had been whimsically busy there" (p. 163). Dr. Hoenikker, Frank, and Newt personify Vonnegut's concern for artistic wonderment, which seems similar to childlike imagination, and how that artistic bent manifests itself in the real world.

Newt, "a midget" by his own explanation, shares the history of his family with John and the reader through an extended letter (p. 18). A self-described outcast and physically childlike, Newt repeatedly notes that his father "wasn't interested in people" (pp. 13–14). That we learn so much about Newt through his stories about his family parallels his own sense of insignificance, fostered by his negligent father. Newt also feels somewhat tortured by his father's obsession with the cat's cradle string trick; Newt explains to John, "No wonder kids grow up crazy," associating the failure of the string trick ("*No damn cat, and no damn cradle*") with the failure of his father (pp. 165–166). Newt contributes the art theme as Frank does, except Newt is a struggling artist who receives pleasure from his art despite negative reactions to it.

While students may find little direct connection between their lives and *Cat's Cradle*'s exploration of science, religion, and art, they certainly all have some interest in the impact of family on their own lives. Rosenblatt (1995) argues for fostering in student readers the ability to make personal connections with literature; the family themes of this novel can serve this crucial element in the development of students as readers, as readers who find meaning and understanding through text. We certainly can ask students to write about Vonnegut's commentary on family, but we can also ask them to write their own original works on their feelings and perceptions of family dynamics in their own lives.

Bokononism—Of Truth and Falsehood, and the Function of Myth

After the dedication page of *Cat's Cradle*, Vonnegut includes two opening statements: "Nothing in this book is true" and a scripture from *The Books of Bokonon* that includes the term "foma," defined on that page as "Harmless untruths" (p. vii). This suggests to me that we might be able to group Vonnegut's science, religion, and art motifs under a broader thematic concern—the nature of truth and falsehood. Central to the novel is the Bokononian religion: "The first sentence in *The Books of Bokonon* is this: 'All of the true things I am about to tell you are shameless lies'" (p. 5).

The writings of Joseph Campbell raise the many notions of "truth," just as Vonnegut does in his fiction. This novel is fertile ground for discussing how society in general and students specifically perceive truth. A statistical truth such as the average family has 2.4 children cannot be found in the real world since we cannot have 0.4 of a child. But that statistic is mathematically true. Students also have dealt for years with the metaphorical truths of fiction and poetry. When the work of Campbell or the writings of Vonnegut force them to consider or reconsider the nature of truth in religious scripture, they are often, however, being pushed into new territories.

In Christian denominations, for example, varying degrees of importance are placed on literal interpretations of the Bible. I have found that students who are comfortable with discussions of metaphorical truth in fiction have a great deal of difficulty making that same consideration with the scripture of their own faith. While these are issues properly left for students to decide on their own, Vonnegut's invented religion and scriptures can be less intimidating avenues for beginning to discuss the essential natures of truth and falsehood, particularly as they are bound by religion, science, and art. At the least, students need to see that truth and falsehood have differing parameters when we change the framework of our references. A religious truth, a scientific truth, and an artistic truth may prove to be false if we change the paradigm.

In *Numbers Games* (2004), I have argued that these perceptions of "truth" are at the heart of the American psyche. The three types of truth I have identified are poetic truth, statistical truth, and historical truth. Students should be asked to explore the nature of truth along with how we determine truth. Let's look at these distinctions briefly here:

- Poetic truth comes to us in the form of literature, particularly fiction and poetry. In this arena of truth, that truth is related to the real world metaphorically. *Cat's Cradle* is a work of fiction, populated by created characters who are not literally people who are in or who have been in this reality. Yet, we pronounce that this novel offers readers many truths about the real world. For students, the novel should be an exercise in seeking those truths along with *how we come to reasonable conclusions about those truths in literary analysis*. What constitutes metaphorical truth (poetic truth), and what process do we use and accept for those conclusions?
- Historical truth captures those people and events that have occurred in this reality, on this planet (or somewhat beyond this planet). This is the world of facts—such as the birth date of a president or the capital of a state. The poetic truth found in a Shakespeare play contrasts in some ways with the historical truth of his biography, but these truths associated with Shakespeare highlight another significant dilemma for students since the historical facts of Shakespeare's biography are filled with as much debate as certainty. How do historians and biographers, for example, reach conclusions about historical facts? Students need to begin to build for themselves the relative nature of determining truth within differing disciplines. The pursuit of truth in literature is both similar to and different from the pursuit of truth in history—or in science. We can help students see the ambiguous nature of historical truth by presenting them with the world of the urban legend; do a simple web search for "Shakespeare" and "Psalm 46," and you will find interesting speculations about clues in the King James Bible that suggest Shakespeare embedded hints in Psalm 46, implying that Shakespeare was one of the translators of the King James version of the Bible. Although this "urban legend" stretches its own parameters (Shakespeare is supposed to have written this at age 46, thus the number of the Psalm and the hints in the 46th words from the beginning and end of the Psalm being "shake" and "spear"—although the counting must be manipulated), this type of debatable history is a ripe argument for exploring just what counts as historical truth. Further, we can ask students to consider how the nature of truth is impacted by the perception of truth; some easily disputed "facts" become more or less truth in the popular view because they are repeated so often—George Washington chopping down the cherry tree or Columbus "discovering" America, for example.
- Statistical truth is the mathematical representation of truth through calculations and numbers. The average person values numbers in a way that he does not value words. Numbers carry the

weight of fact and truth that suggests objectivity while words feel subjective. As well, we tend to value statistical averages while essentially ignoring other statistical measures such as modes or medians. One statistical situation I often present to students is this: There are 14 people in a room; when they take out their money and add the amounts, we discover that the group has $140. How much money does the average person in the group have? The answer, of course, is $10. That average is a statistical truth. I then tell the students that one person in the group had $140 while the other 13 had no money, asking them to consider the contrast between the statistical truth of the average and the reality of the group. I also add that the modality is $0; thus, the mode of that group is closer to the reality than the average—although the average and the mode are both statistically true.

The distinctions I have offered are somewhat arbitrary. Another way to approach truth, particularly as it is offered through literature, is to turn to Campbell's *The Power of Myth,* where he discusses the four functions of myth (thus literature and its truths). Campbell (1988) sees these four functions as mystical, cosmological, sociological, and pedagogical. He considers the mystical function as one of "awe" and "mystery," what many of us might associate with religion and faith (p. 31). Part of Campbell's argument is that modern humans have lost a great deal of that awe because so much of the world has been explained by science. A second function, cosmological, is the world of science, where we look for those stories that explain the physical world in ways that we are unable to explain otherwise; Campbell notes how science can explain fire technically, but that technical information "doesn't tell me a thing" (p. 31). The third function of myth for Campbell is sociological—"supporting and validating a certain social order" (p. 31). In a more complex sense, some myth in the form of literature confronts the status quo, suggesting alternative social orders. Campbell's fourth function is pedagogical, which he describes as showing humans "how to live a human lifetime under any circumstances" (p. 31). These functions of myth, of storytelling through literature, provide students a structure for discussing how *Cat's Cradle* addresses truth (and falsehood): Does the novel fill the reader with awe and wonder about existence? Does the novel address the truths of the physical world that science explores? Does the novel confront or support any existing or possible social order? Does the novel help the reader know how to live in the world that the reader has been handed?

Ultimately, studying *Cat's Cradle* can be about what we consider to be truth and what we consider to be false—along with how we come to those conclusions within different paradigms. Counting and numbers seem to make the urban legend about Shakespeare and Psalm 46 true, but is that appearance of truth supported by our tendency to trust numbers? These discussions of truth can begin with Vonnegut's poetic truths in his novel; then we can ask students to make these discoveries in their own lives while they are experiencing those transition years that leave the black and white world of childhood behind for the very gray world of adulthood.

Cat's Cradle as Symbolic Motif

The circle—from the wedding band to the twisted circle that forms the infinity symbol—is infused with meaning in religion, philosophy, art, and literature across many years and many cultures. Like Dr. Hoenikker, we can take a circle of string, lace it through our fingers, and produce what is called a "cat's cradle." For Dr. Hoenikker's son Newt, this children's game becomes a lesson in the falsehood of symbolism—"*No damn cat, and no damn cradle*" (p. 166). Newt within the novel becomes disillusioned by the contrast between literal and metaphorical truth. As well, Vonnegut creates his own sort of literary cat's cradle by weaving the cat's cradle motif in the form of circles, lattice images, and string references throughout the novel, creating symbolic value in the image for both the characters and the reader.

The value of the circle carries some inherent ambiguities since, as Marvin (2002) notes, the circle can be nothing, designated by zero, or infinity, the endless line; further, Marvin adds, "Circles traditionally symbolize wholeness, because the line has no end, and emptiness, because the area inside is empty" (p. 90). The cat's cradle motif, then, poses these problems for students as readers who work to determine how Vonnegut is portraying the motif throughout the novel. The essential detail of the circle motif through the cat's cradle in the novel is Marvin's connection between the string game "becom[ing] a symbol of our ability to shape the world around us and by shaping it, giv[ing] it meaning" (p. 90). The cat's cradle, then, becomes a simple form of art, a creation: "The point of making a cat's cradle is not to create a real cat and a real cradle, but to have fun making something out of nothing" (Marvin, p. 91). Newt's character and the tenants of the Bokononian religion warn the reader about confusing the literal with the metaphorical.

For students, this motif offers a wonderful opportunity to make distinctions between how elements in literature work within the novel as compared with how they work for the reader. Newt's character can be analyzed for how Dr. Hoenikker's cat's cradle impacts Newt in his life, but the motifs running throughout the novel create meaning for the reader; those meanings are not necessarily related. Let's look at some of the ways this motif manifests itself throughout the novel:

- *The cat's cradle itself:* Chapter Five introduces the reader to Newt's letter to John, the narrator, and Dr. Hoenikker's fascination with the cat's cradle. Here the reader discovers the source of the string; it had been wrapped around a science fiction novel about the end of the world. Newt's letter adds: "Making the cat's cradle was the closet I ever saw my father come to playing what anybody else would call a game" (p. 11). Here, we can ask students how the cat's cradle contributes to the characterizations of Newt and Dr. Hoenikker.
- *String:* In Chapter 35, John discusses Frank Hoenikker with Jack, who says, "I'm still trying to pull the strings of my life back together again" (p. 74). The cat's cradle motif is supported by string references, this one suggesting the need in people to tie things together, to gain some control over their lives.
- *Lattice image:* Frank's house in Chapter 74 includes a terrace: "It was a cunning lattice of very light steel posts and beams" (p. 163). The end of this chapter includes Newt's lament that the cat's cradle string game is "'nothing but a bunch of X's between somebody's hands'" (pp. 165–166).

While the many ways in which the cat's cradle motif is woven through the novel present the reader with ambiguities and contradictions that might lead to understanding, Marvin (2002) ties this motif into a perceptive bow: "[T]he symbol of the cat's cradle allows Vonnegut to explore the underlying similarities between activities as diverse as art, science, religion, and sociology"—thus the many thematic elements of the entire novel. Just as Newt rages against the cat's cradle that has no cat, has no cradle, the reader of *Cat's Cradle* may eventually discover a novel about a religion that is no religion at all.

Cat's Cradle, the Book of Jonah, and *Moby-Dick*

Vonnegut as experimental or postmodern novelist provides for our English courses works that are both rejections of a certain status quo and an embodiment of those traditional assumptions about literature. As I have discussed in earlier chapters, Vonnegut's works tend to manipulate narration, characterization, plot, and other elements that we address in academic settings. His work also challenges neat classifications of genre and New Critical stances of interpretation. For traditionalists, such as those in Harold Bloom's camp, experimental works are often declared inferior when they do not conform to the criteria that the literary work itself rejects. When we are preparing students for somewhat traditional academic settings, we might avoid works such as Vonnegut's because we feel the need to prepare them for the traditional academic world that we know exists—not necessarily for an academic world we might prefer. As I offered with *Slaughterhouse-Five,* relatively traditional approaches to *Cat's Cradle* can help teachers avoid censoring the book out of such a fear.

Cat's Cradle can be taught either in conjunction with Herman Melville's *Moby-Dick* or as a follow-up or precursor to the classic American novel. Marvin (2002) and other critics acknowledge that this novel by Vonnegut clearly echoes *Moby-Dick* and the biblical Book of Jonah. Students may study *Cat's Cradle* as a sustained allusion to Melville's work and to the Book of Jonah. These questions can guide such a study of the novel (see Marvin, 2002):

- *The New Oxford Annotated Bible* (1991) states that "[t]he book of Jonah is unique among the prophetic books" (p. 1186 OT). The book is called "a prose narrative about the prophet himself," who is "recalcitrant" and "sulks when his hearers repent" (p. 1186 OT). Students should be asked to analyze the Book of Jonah along with explaining how the biblical text informs Vonnegut's opening line: "Call me Jonah" (p. 1). How are the roles of the biblical Jonah and the novel's narrator similar? Different? How does the extended biblical allusion to the prophet Jonah contribute to the religious themes of the novel. The brevity of this Biblical book allows for quick and manageable discussions in our classes; it also helps reinforce the need for most students of English-language literature to be well versed in Christian mythology, regardless of the students' faith.
- The same first line that alludes to the Book of Jonah also alludes to the opening line of Melville's *Moby-Dick.* Marvin (2002) believes that the *Moby-Dick* allusions continue into Chapter 94 where Mount McCabe is described with two whale references and a harpoon reference (p. 210). How do *Cat's Cradle* and *Moby-Dick* approach similar themes? The narrative similarities are also paralleled by the two novels' concern for the relationship between humans and nature.

"Vonnegut taps into the symbolic power of the Book of Jonah and *Moby-Dick* in order to warn his readers against trying to control forces that they can never understand," concludes Marvin (2002, p. 95). Here, we might use Vonnegut's own string image to suggest that allusion is a primary technique Vonnegut as postmodern novelist uses to tie together the many seemingly disparate elements of his novel—although we might all as teachers, students, and readers be wise to remain cautious in making any sweeping conclusions just in case Vonnegut proves to be impossible to decipher.

ENTRY POINTS AND CONNECTIONS

"The Luckiest," Ben Folds, *Rockin' the Suburbs*

The Power of Myth, Joseph Campbell with Bill Moyers

"Anxiety," Grace Paley

"Fire and Ice," Robert Frost

"It's the End of the World as We Know It (And I Feel Fine)," REM, *Document*

Death of a Salesman, Arthur Miller

A Raisin in the Sun, Lorraine Hansberry

The Glass Menagerie, Tennessee Williams

Chapter Five

Player Piano and *Galapagos*

The Evolution of Science and Technology

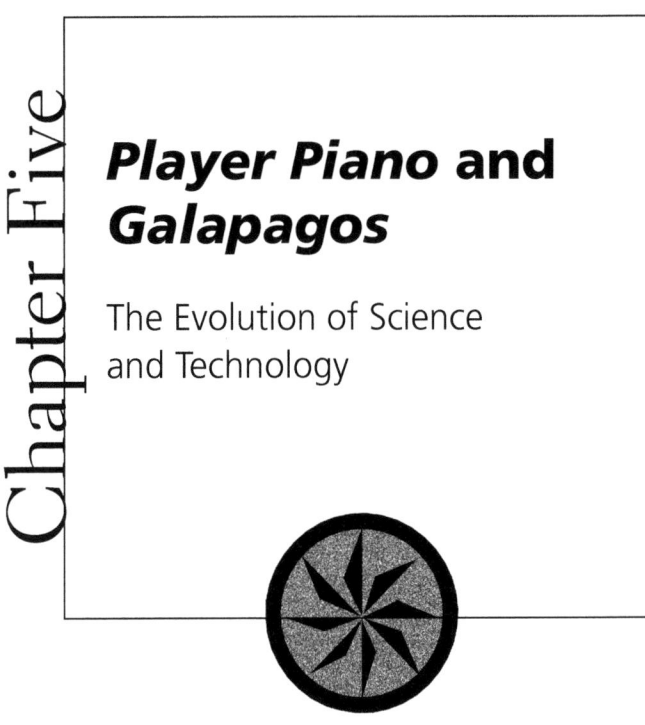

More than a decade after his first novel, *Player Piano* (1952), Vonnegut wrote a piece on science fiction for *The New York Times Book Review* (later included in *Wampeters, Foma & Granfalloons*) confessing:

> I have been a soreheaded occupant of a file drawer labeled "science fiction" ever since, and I would like out, particularly since so many serious critics regularly mistake the drawer for a urinal. (p. 1)

The essay highlights not only Vonnegut's antagonistic relationship with being included in the sci-fi genre but also the second-class status of the genre. When we consider bringing Vonnegut into the English classroom, we are immediately confronted with not only the traditional discounting of science fiction literature, but also our own perceptions of the genre and our own biases concerning the broader humanities field as it contrasts with the sciences.

Vonnegut continues in "Science Fiction" to criticize the somewhat arbitrary classification of writing as science fiction by noting that any writer who "[writes] about people and machines" or "notice[s] technology" is labeled as a science fiction writer. He attributes this dynamic to the attitude of the English literature field: "English majors are encouraged, I know, to hate chemistry and physics. . . . So it is natural for them to despise science fiction" (pp. 1–2). This brief essay expresses Vonnegut's own displeasure at being considered a science fiction writer and with the cultish nature of science fiction writers themselves, even calling science fiction "comic books without pictures" (p. 3). The culmination of Vonnegut's rant is extremely interesting since he notes that many treasured authors could be classified as science fiction writers if we wished to do so: "Boomers of science fiction might reply, 'Ha! Orwell and Ellison and Flaubert and Kafka are science-fiction writers too!'" (p. 4).

With these essential concerns in mind, we will discuss here two of Vonnegut's novels that are most centrally concerned with science, *Player Piano* and *Galapagos*. We will look at how these novels in many ways conform to the assumptions about science fiction as a genre while also moving beyond those parameters; *Player Piano* provides a sharp assessment of technology, while *Galapagos* dramatizes Charles Darwin's evolutionary theory. I will begin this chapter, however, by looking at how English teachers can address their own perceptions of science and science fiction before adding these novels to the curriculum.

CONNECTION

Gregor Samsa wakes one morning to discover that he is an insect; thus begins one of the most recognizable works of fiction, the novella *The Metamorphosis* by Franz Kafka. In conjunction with Vonnegut's essay, "Science Fiction," or the novels discussed in this chapter, students can debate whether or not Kafka's story is science fiction. This debate can help students clarify their own understanding of genre in general and of sci-fi specifically. The debate might also lead to students making some fine distinctions between sci-fi and fantasy as well—a distinction that die-hard fans believe is sacred. A search on the Internet will uncover arguments over Harry Potter books receiving sci-fi awards. This discussion, however, will certainly allow teachers and students to look closely at assumptions about literature and the quality of literature as well.

Louise Rosenblatt and the Teaching of Literature—Teacher Assumptions and Biases within the Humanities and Sciences

"Teachers of literature and the arts often think of themselves as saving the student from the stultifying effects of our present scientific age," explains Rosenblatt (1995) in her *Literature as Exploration* (p. 127). Echoing in some ways Vonnegut's theory about the tendency to discount science fiction literature in English courses, Rosenblatt's work provides teachers of English with an opportunity to consider our own attitudes about science and about science fiction. While I cannot fully substitute for Rosenblatt's seminal work on teaching and reading literature, I want to outline here briefly the points she makes that help teachers of English rectify the tension that exists between the arts and the sciences.

ENTRY POINT

While we as teachers will benefit from reflecting on our attitudes toward science and science fiction, we can also bring that reflection to the classroom for our students. Many artists offer their argument as to the value of nature or emotion over the precision of science. Three brief works that work well with students are Coldplay's song "The Scientist" as an opening activity to reading Wordsworth's "The Tables Turned" and e. e. cummings's "since feeling is first." All of these works raise issues about the tension between emotion and thought.

As teachers of English, we should clarify our own perceptions of and attitudes about science. Rosenblatt (1995) warns that we commonly blame science for consequences more aptly attributed to "the practical, materialistic emphasis of our society" (p. 127). As Vonnegut might argue, the use and misuse of science (such as Vonnegut dramatizes in *Player Piano*) in the name of other pursuits (materialistic or capitalistic, for example) do not reveal science as an evil. The flaw is in the use. Do we as teachers of English have this misconception? And do we intentionally or unintentionally foster that attitude in our classes? Rosenblatt asks us to explore these questions, and I feel we must if we intend to include science fiction and Vonnegut in our classes.

Rosenblatt (1995) also makes a precise and revealing observation about our basic distinction between science and art; we associate laws and generalizing with science while praising the arts for "seek[ing] to individualize rather than to generalize" (p. 129). Further, as I have argued elsewhere (Thomas, 2004), Rosenblatt identifies the negative impact behaviorism and "technical jargon" have had on the perception of science, especially among those of us in the humanities (p. 129). As a member of an e-mail group, I have witnessed the science community openly denigrate the humanities with broad and unfair generalizations, just as I feel many in the humanities do to the sciences.

First, for ourselves as scholars and as teachers, we must begin to define science and scientific inquiry, looking closely for how science and the arts are similar: "The artist orders and classifies data offered by life as much as science does," explains Rosenblatt (1995, p. 131). A more complex view of science—that scientific findings are tentative and evolving—helps us when we are faced with the ongoing and polarizing debates that enter our classroom—such as the evolution debate I will address later in this chapter. This clarification about science is key:

> Scientific knowledge is essentially a cooperative product. Only as a fact or theory is tested and verified by many competent minds, often widely scattered in time and space, does that fact or theory come to be accepted. (Rosenblatt, p. 132)

Couldn't this exact explanation be made for how we come to analytical conclusions about literature or any art?

Now, if we are dedicated to developing English courses that support a symbiotic relationship between the arts and sciences (including adding Vonnegut's works and other works of science fiction), we may wish to embrace the characteristics offered by Rosenblatt (1995), which I will outline here:

- English teachers should support the broad concept of "scrupulous inquiry," which is "flexible" but rigorous (p. 136). This, of course, is the essential nature of reaching supported literary interpretations, of agreeing upon the characteristics of effective writing, for example.
- English teachers should avoid "a dogmatic framework on the concept of human nature" (p. 136).
- English teachers should encourage and model skepticism, particularly in the face of "conventional assumptions" (p. 136).
- English teachers should not allow students to "fall back on pat, stereotyped formulas" (p. 136).
- English teachers should foster in students an awareness of and appreciation for the "complexity of human behavior" (p. 136).
- English teachers should teach students that inquiry is a systematic process that is collaborative and organic.

Bringing Vonnegut and science fiction into our classrooms provides English teachers with an opportunity to reflect upon our own understanding of science. Further, if we begin to push our own assumptions and conceptions of science—and its relationship with the arts—then we can expand those same discussions in our classes. For me, bringing Vonnegut and science into our English classes becomes ultimately an authentic experience with the precise meanings of words. Much of a scientific or more broadly a scholarly conversation depends greatly on all members of that dialogue clarifying and appreciating the terminology used. As I have offered before (Thomas, 2005a), students must be asked to confront terms such as "theory," "belief," and even "science" if they are to reach the level of sophistication required to make positive contributions in a democracy of educated people.

Dystopian Novel Unit—Sci-Fi Novels and Movies

"*Player Piano* is set the future after a fictional third world war," explains Marvin (2002), adding, "Critics have often compared [the novel] with Aldous Huxley's *Brave New World* and George Orwell's *1984*," both often included in reading lists in our high schools and colleges despite their science fiction qualities (p. 25). Marvin then describes these three novels as within the utopian tradition of speculative or science fiction novels. Reviewers and critics (Mustazza, 1994) tend to categorize *Galapagos* as distinct in some ways from the classic utopian novel but essentially working within and against that paradigm. Strictly stated, Vonnegut's two novels are dystopian in that they uncover horrific futures in many respects. Whether we call this type of science fiction utopian or dystopian, a novel unit that combines speculative fiction dealing with the future societies of humans is often enthusiastically embraced by high school and college students. This unit also allows introducing students to one or more engaging science fiction movies related to some of the most highly regarded science fiction novels.

ENTRY POINT

An obvious and classic entry point for this unit is Sir Thomas More's *Utopia*—the source for the terms "utopia" and "dystopia." Utopias are generally described as ideal societies, while dystopias are societies that may appear ideal but are in fact dehumanizing and essentially hells on earth. More's classic work, easily accessed on-line or in inexpensive book form, offers readers both a description of an ideal world that could work and an argument that ideal societies are attainable. For students, this work allows them to debate each idea: What would an ideal society entail? Can an ideal society exist?

CONNECTION

Students can benefit greatly from authentic contributions to the wider debates within the field of literature. In *Writing with Intent,* Margaret Atwood (2005) offers three essays that confront the arguments about science fiction and dystopian literature—"Writing Utopia" (about *The Handmaid's Tale*), "*The Birthday of the World and Other Stories* by Ursula K. Le Guin" (a review that wrestles with genre), and "George Orwell: Some Personal Connections" (a wonderful essay that fits well with this unit or with Orwell's works). In "Writing Utopia," for instance, Atwood offers an excellent discussion of her own views about science fiction writing as contrasted with speculative fiction, along with offering characteristics for both. She also discusses the nature of utopian and dystopian literature. All three of these essays are authentic arguments—pieces published by a living author—and they expose students to a highly nuanced and scholarly discussion that challenges their assumptions. Atwood's guidelines for science fiction, speculative fiction, and utopian/dystopian literature can be used as the basis for critiquing the novels in this unit.

Along with Vonnegut's *Player Piano* and *Galapagos*—works that offer distinct explorations of future societies—students can be assigned a number of high-quality novels that confront utopias and dystopias. I want to suggest novels that might be effective companions in this unit. First, let me add that all of these novels go beyond speculating on the future of humanity and our societies; they also offer sharp criticisms of current aspects of those societies within which each writer lived. Novels appropriate for this unit include the following:

- *1984,* George Orwell—This work has become *the* classic sci-fi novel within relatively traditional curriculums. Orwell simply transposed slightly the year 1948 and wrote a harsh indictment of his own society. Although the work appears to be a futuristic society, Orwell was not predicting the state of the world in 1984 but was protesting qualities of his own society. This work introduced the term "Big Brother" into the popular vocabulary. The dark nature of the book and the language make teaching *1984* similar in many ways to teaching Hawthorne's *The Scarlet Letter* in that students often enjoy discussing these books but balk at the actual reading of the novel.
- *Brave New World,* Aldous Huxley—Often taught and well regarded, much like *1984,* this sci-fi classic tends to capture the imagination of students both as a good read and as a source of vigorous discussion more readily than *1984.* Huxley's novel is more science oriented than *1984,* making this novel an excellent companion to Vonnegut's *Player Piano* since they both raise concerns about the uses of science and technology to oppress humanity even as they appear to improve the human condition. The sexual and procreation issues in *Brave New World* are central themes of the work, but the novel poses few problems with potential censorship challenges.
- *The Handmaid's Tale* and *Oryx and Crake,* Margaret Atwood—Canadian novelist Atwood has established herself as a highly regarded contemporary novelist who garners critical praise and

popular success—notably with works that are traditional literary fiction and works that are embraced by the sci-fi community. *The Handmaid's Tale* is a speculative novel much like *1984* in that it has greater political overtones than scientific or technological ones. This work is Atwood's satirical dark look at the threat she perceived from a growing conservative and religious movement that has been seeking political power in the U.S. for over two decades. *The Handmaid's Tale* explores fertility and procreation issues as does *Brave New World*. Having taught this novel for many years, I feel that it has been one of the most successful novels I have ever introduced to my classroom. In 2003, Atwood published *Oryx and Crake*, a post-apocalyptic novel that matches well with Vonnegut's *Galapagos*.

- *Fahrenheit 451,* Ray Bradbury—Bradbury is a giant in the field of science fiction, a writer mentioned often and respected by Vonnegut. This classic novel deals with a futuristic society at war with books. The science fiction and speculative themes fit well with Vonnegut's novels and the other novels mentioned here; additionally, the novel's themes dealing with literature and censorship make this novel ideal for our classrooms. Many works of literature raise issues concerning the power of language along with the power held by those who control language. *Fahrenheit 451* shares with Atwood's *The Handmaid's Tale* several issues, including the language motif (the importance of language and who control language and literature, including religious texts) and the dangers posed by an authoritarian government that offers peace and tranquility at a great cost to individual freedom.
- *A Clockwork Orange,* Anthony Burgess—This novel (and the popular movie version) offers a highly disturbing futuristic society; the work confronts the reader with intense violence. *A Clockwork Orange* is an ideal companion to Vonnegut's works in many ways. Burgess's technique is similar to Vonnegut's in a number of works, and he deals with the threat of behavioral psychology along with raising questions about the nature of human free will.

CONNECTION

Sci-fi movies have cult-like followings. Assigning a sci-fi movie as part of this unit can be an effective instructional strategy. A number of these novels have high-quality movie versions—*1984, Fahrenheit 451, A Clockwork Orange*. Many other sci-fi movies are respected by movie critics and sci-fi communities. I recommend bringing into the class the original *Planet of the Apes* and *Soylent Green* as engaging and dynamic examples of the themes and characteristics common to utopian/dystopian novels.

Using utopian/dystopian sci-fi novels in our English classes provides an opportunity for a number of goals and objectives, along with instructional strategies, that would work well with all of these works or any of these works individually—or with either of the Vonnegut novels addressed in this chapter. Let's look at some here:

- Since many of these works deal directly and indirectly with the role of government, this unit allows students to explore how governments support and oppress humans in many different forms and across cultures and history. Vonnegut's novels often address the power of organizations (not just government, as in the power of a corporation in *Player Piano*) along with the likelihood that organizations will oppress; other novels in this section address government directly, such as *The Handmaid's Tale* and *1984*.
- Naturally, this unit raises issues about the positive and negative impacts of science and technology. Vonnegut's work should never be viewed as anti-science or anti-technology; I would argue that most of these works show that science and technology are often weapons of greater forces when they fail humanity. Modern students are awash in technology—cell phones, iPods, computers—therefore, these works are valuable windows to reconsidering science and technology by a generation deeply intertwined with both.
- Popular themes in Vonnegut's works—free will and determinism—are central to most sci-fi novels addressing utopias/dystopias. Students will find these arguments engaging during their transition from childhood into adulthood—when the weight of adult responsibility begins to become real. Many of the novels discussed above, including Vonnegut's novels, address the question of free will ambiguously, leaving readers ample evidence to argue many angles of the debate.
- The novels in this unit offer two divergent purposes simultaneously—sharp criticisms of humanity in the present (although that "present" may sometimes narrowly encompass the historical era of the writer) and varying degrees of warnings about the future state of humankind. Both of these are ripe for discussion in our classes. Students should be asked how these works highlight flaws and weaknesses in our societies now; then, they should be asked to identify and evaluate the apparent warnings these works offer about our future. This last concern can lead to students speculating about possible action humanity

can take to avoid these dangers as well as considering how we can address current flaws in our contemporary world. I have often tried to raise students' awareness concerning humanity's ability to see fairly clearly the flaws in past societies—from the naïve belief of primitive cultures that fire came to humans as a gift from God (instead of being a relatively easily produced natural phenomenon) to the corrupt use of biblical texts to justify slavery in early America—while also maintaining and vigorously supporting current behaviors that are just as flawed. In other words, humans have great difficulty seeing clearly those things that are closest to our eyes. Sci-fi novels allow current foibles dressed in speculative clothes to be more easily analyzed.

CONNECTION

If we begin asking students to consider questions about the nature of existence, we are shepherding them into the world of philosophy—Does each human have free will? What is the nature of paradise (or heaven)? What is the nature of life on earth (or hell)? Literature addresses these concerns in dramatic ways; one of the most famous philosophical works is Jean-Paul Sartre's *No Exit*—a work notable for dramatizing Sartre's version of existential philosophy. The play shows the audience that hell is other people, that hell is not some mythological place beyond this life but life itself here on earth. Many utopian and dystopian works of science fiction portray hellish societies that parallel Sartre's argument. Particularly if we bring sci-fi movies with post-apocalyptic themes into our classes, students begin to identify the "hell is on earth" motif; for many, this message is exclusively negative. Yet, within existential philosophy, that hell is life on earth is simply a fact of existence—neither good nor bad. This debate is a valuable and enlightening one for high school and college students.

One or both of Vonnegut's novels *Player Piano* and *Galapagos* can serve as excellent anchors for a unit on utopian and dystopian literature. While Vonnegut is often characterized as a science fiction writer, I feel that these two works represent the essential science fiction nature of his work well, because of their similarities and their differences. Let's now turn to how we might implement each of these novels if we choose to use them as single-novel units in our classes.

Player Piano—Satire and Sci-Fi

"*Player Piano* is a satire on post-World War II America," argues Marvin (2002, p. 25). I might add that this satire grows from Vonnegut's experiences during his work for the General Electric Corporation; his satire of the corporate world (and the science inherent in that world) is a microcosm of his larger satire of American values at mid-twentieth century: "an uncritical faith in technology and 'progress,' an insatiable desire for material possessions, a lack of interest in politics, and a deliberate effort to encourage women to leave the work force" (Marvin, p. 26). The complex and overlapping nature of Vonnegut's satire in this novel can be a significant challenge to high school and college students, creating an ideal situation for students to research many overlapping areas related during their study of the novel.

Futuristic works of science fiction are often grounded in details of the contemporary society of the author—although the nature of science fiction masks those details. Vonnegut clearly parodies many aspects of 1940s and 1950s America in *Player Piano,* but those decades are quite foreign to early twenty-first century students in our English courses. This novel study should ask students to research many aspects of mid-twentieth century America. Interesting sources of that research can include how more recent portrayals of that period characterize it—TV shows such as "Happy Days" or movies such as *Pleasantville.* Students will need to gather a variety of sources on mid-1900s America before they can identify the satire in Vonnegut's work.

Another target of satire foreign to high school and college students is the corporate world as dramatized and parodied by Vonnegut. The GE of Vonnegut's early career had some unique qualities, but the corporate world satirized by Vonnegut at mid-twentieth century remains relevant today in the broader concepts. In some way or other, our students will soon be entering that corporate world, and *Player Piano* can be one window—a highly critical window—into the world of business. Vonnegut's satire addresses the hierarchy of corporations, the role of technology in corporations, the assumptions about and complete faith in capitalism within corporations, and gender issues in the corporate world. The gender issues are particularly interesting since students should analyze not only how gender matters in the mid-1950s but also how gender matters today (they need to ask themselves how much things have or have not changed).

Further satire in the novel addresses what I would consider highly specific concepts and practices, notably behavioral psychology, statistics (along with IQ measurements), and capitalism. Many of these forces work so closely with daily American life that few people can see them or separate them from broader assumptions about life in general. Here, we have a wonderful opportunity to help students develop sophisticated knowledge of what such terms mean along with asking them to begin to analyze skeptically how they influence and even control our lives. Of particular interest to students in high school and college is how educational and intellectual measurements (specifically SAT scores and IQ testing) label and dictate young people's lives. In *Player Piano,* people's lives are dictated through government mandates based on IQ scores; students can readily see that the *de jure* nature of this parallels a *de facto* existence of such for their lives—SAT scores greatly influence college entrance and thus future professions.

CONNECTIONS

Stephen Jay Gould's *The Mismeasure of Man* and Alfie Kohn's *The Case Against Standardized Testing* might be of great interest in part or as outside assignments for a number of our students. Gould's work deals with the history of scientific efforts to quantify intelligence, showing the inherent flaws in that pursuit, whether it be measuring the volume of the human skull or asking students a series of multiple-choice questions. Students can learn a great deal about the nature of science and of measurement in Gould's famous work that was re-issued after a resurgence of the IQ and bell-curve debate sparked by the controversial *The Bell Curve* by Richard Herrnstein and Charles Murray. Related to this debate is the tension all educators are experiencing concerning testing of students and evaluations of teachers and schools. An early and persistent critic of excessive and misguided testing of students is Alfie Kohn; his *The Case Against Standardized Testing* is a brief and manageable argument that students certainly would find enlightening.

Beyond discussions of Vonnegut's satire of America, students can be led to create satires of their lives, including current characteristics of the government, their schools, and the broader pop culture of America. Satire as a critical lens is one of the most powerful tools for writers of any genre, and it is essential that our students gain sophistication in their reading of satire and in their ability to use satire in their own writing.

Player Piano—The Myth of Proteus

When I began my career as a high school English teacher, I taught a couple of classes in senior English, or British literature. Part of that curriculum included extensive coverage and testing of Greek and Roman mythology. Anyone who happened to drop by during this unit would have been certain that the only thing that mattered in senior English was an extensive listing of Greek and Roman gods! Soon I discovered that this sort of approach was tremendously ineffective and counterproductive. Students scored poorly on the selected-response tests (as offered by my colleagues and administered to all seniors in English) and came to hate mythology.

Issues and debates about the teaching of mythology in our English classes are essentially parallel to most of the debates about the teaching of English. We have ample evidence that teaching Greek and Roman mythology as a goal of instruction in our courses is less than effective. We also know, as English teachers, that students can benefit greatly from a knowledge of mythology as they develop as readers and literary scholars. The problem is how to infuse effectively our English courses with mythology. Many modern works, even nontraditional works such as Vonnegut's, still maintain the literary tradition of using allusion and mythological patterns as central aspects of the work. Joseph Campbell argues that all literature and creative works share basic mythological patterns; he embraces a Jungian concept of the collective unconscious that explains how all humans share basic patterns of story and myth. Whether we agree with Campbell's argument or not, we know that English language literature of all genres often requires that readers have some level of knowledge of classical mythology.

ENTRY POINT

If we feel the need to convince our students that mythology and mythological patterns are valuable, we should use Joseph Campbell's *The Hero with a Thousand Faces* as an entry point into mythological patterns in literature and religious texts. Campbell's work introduces students to the ten-step journey of the hero. His ability to express complex content so that students at nearly any level can grasp his premise and his wealth of knowledge concerning mythology and world religions makes Campbell's book extremely rewarding in the classroom. Students will find that they can apply Campbell's "stages" to books, the Bible, movies, TV series, and even comic books—all enjoyable and productive activities for our classes.

Vonnegut's *Player Piano* introduces students to Homer's *Odyssey* and the myth of Proteus (see www.theoi.com/Pontios/Proteus.html for a quick guide to the myth and related information on Greek mythology). Relating the novel's main character, Paul Proteus, to the myth of Proteus solves one problem with addressing classic mythology; students see the direct relevance of studying the myth of Proteus since it is integral to the novel. Traditional approaches to teaching mythology have often been isolated, thus ineffective. As well, the use of Proteus by Vonnegut confronts readers with something of a dilemma since it isn't completely clear how Proteus contributes to our understanding of Paul.

Marvin (2002) notes that Proteus is "a sea monster that can change his shape at will. . . . In a sense, Paul Proteus also lacks a definite shape" (p. 29). Students can begin by exploring how Paul fits this pattern throughout the novel—Does Paul suffer from a lack of identity? How does Vonnegut portray Paul's shifting identity in the novel? Marvin also notes that Paul differs from the mythological sea monster, however, in terms of what causes the shape shifting. Proteus uses this power as he wishes; "Paul's changes are forced on him by circumstances beyond his control," adds Marvin (p. 30). The use of mythology here allows Vonnegut to raise the theme of free will again.

CONNECTION

A wonderful movie that makes its own commentary on the documentary form, Woody Allen's *Zelig*, details the life of the main character, Leonard Zelig, a human chameleon. Zelig, Proteus, and Paul Proteus of Vonnegut's novel all shape shift. Zelig and Paul have those changes forced upon them by the nature of their environment. Paul seems to be the victim of a highly mechanized society; Zelig's shifting shape appears to be the manifestation of his own psychoses brought on by his feelings of alienation in a modern world. This movie is an excellent source for discussion of the shape-changing motif, but it also satirizes American society and comments upon the documentary movie form.

Integrating lessons on classical mythology with studying *Player Piano* fulfills many of our goals concerning authentic teaching and learning of reading and writing in high school and college English courses. Students are exposed to a rich curriculum including the study of the novel form, considerations of genre, introduction to classical mythology, Jungian arguments about the collective unconscious, literary and mythological patterns, and rich reading and writing experiences.

Player Piano—America's View of Artists and Women

Vonnegut has been criticized negatively many times throughout his career for creating flat characters, for writing mere genre fiction, and for failing to address feminist issues (or at least having inadequate female characters in his works). As well, many critics and readers tend to focus on Vonnegut's concern for science and technology to the exclusion of the other issues his works address. In *Player Piano,* Vonnegut does deal with the role of women in society, and he also includes an extended theme about art, creativity, and artists as well. Since these topics are often ignored when studying Vonnegut, I believe we should emphasize them here and in his other works also.

Marvin (2002) explains about Paul's wife: "Anita is a beautiful, ambitious woman who must channel her ambition into promoting her husband's career because the system does not allow women to pursue their own careers" (p. 31). Contemporary students might find this element of the novel to be dated, arguing that Vonnegut's depiction of women in this futuristic society is merely a criticism of mid-twentieth century American chauvinism. Anita is a significant character in this novel; her role raises for readers a necessary consideration of just how far women have advanced in contemporary America, particularly in the corporate world. Is the depiction of women in *Player Piano* merely a depiction of overt sexism in our past, or does her character help readers see that subtle sexism still remains?

The cultural alienation of Anita from a career is paralleled in many respects with the mechanical nature of the marriage between Paul and Anita, asking readers to reflect on the role of women in marriage. These motifs dealing with the roles of women in business, society, and marriage are juxtaposed in this exchange between Paul and Anita:

> "No, no. You've got something the tests and machines will never be able to measure: you're artistic. That's one of the tragedies of our times, that no machine has ever been built that can recognize that quality, appreciate it, foster it, sympathize with it." [stated Paul]
>
> "It is," said Anita sadly. "It is, it is."
>
> "I love you, Anita."
>
> "I love *you,* Paul." (pp. 178–179)

Vonnegut's commentary on the role of women and the role of art and artists is dramatized briefly here; further, the mechanistic refrain—"I love *you*"—that runs throughout the novel punctuates both the reduced status of Anita and the hollow nature of marriage—all seemingly brought about by the dehumanizing aspects easily recognized in American society during the mid-twentieth century and today.

While students can focus on Anita to explore Vonnegut's themes about women and art, the novel includes many other characters and situations addressing these motifs as well. "For most of his life, Finnerty did not take time to consider the social consequences of his creativity," explains Marvin (2002, p. 31). Finnerty serves as a rebellious and creative contrast to Paul's tendency to conform throughout the novel. Also serving as a contrast is Lawson Shepherd, whose competitive nature parallels Anita's. With the interconnected stories involving Paul, Anita, Finnerty, and Shepherd, *Player Piano* cannot be accused of ignoring the status of women; the novel is also clearly much more than a criticism of technology gone mad.

Vonnegut's narrative weaves a complex dynamic among distinct characters. That story shows the tensions that exist within intimate relationships—marriage, lovers, friendship—and within larger societal contexts—business, underground societies. Those tensions involve the impact technology and science have on art, and vice versa. Any human society at any time struggles with conflicts that force each person to make choices, often choices between intellect and emotion. Has the society's devaluing of women and artists reduced Anita to living her life through her husband? And how should the reader respond to Anita for adopting the parameters for success of her society, for sacrificing her marriage for a partner who fits the corporate mold for success? Students should be asked to identify these same concerns in our society today.

Player Piano—Symbolism in an American Novel

"Bud's mentality was one that had been remarked upon as being peculiarly American since the nation had been born—the restless, erratic insight and imagination of the gadgeteer"—this quotation from the novel establishes *Player Piano* as much more than simply a science fiction novel that offers a derivative complaint about the dangers of technology (pp. 4–5). Vonnegut's novel stands in a rich American tradition that can be traced to major American literary figures mentioned later in the novel—"'You know about Thoreau and Emerson?'" (p. 143). In "Civil Disobedience" and *Walden,* Thoreau mentions "machine" in his most critical sentences and warns about the dangers of becoming wed to the speed and ease of train travel. Through the symbolism of the player piano in his novel, Vonnegut joins that tradition of American literature that is most skeptical of the advantages of technological advances.

- -

CONNECTION

Henry David Thoreau offers both "Civil Disobedience," and *Walden,* which speak skeptically about technology and the fear that such advances reduce humans to machines. While Vonnegut's works feel futuristic to most readers, Thoreau's discussions may strike students as silly since the technology he is discussing seems antiquated to modern readers. This combination of readings, however, will help students see that the *concepts* are similar—and that the technology itself is not as important as the impact the advances have on humans. Even when Thoreau discusses the dangers of people committing themselves too fully to their work, he warns that "[h]e has no time to be any thing but a machine" (p. 109). Thoreau's fears and concerns are echoed by Vonnegut—although the works use contrasting styles and genres. When Thoreau cries, "But lo! men have become the tools of their tools," students are apt to see that message dramatized in Vonnegut's novel when the characters in *Player Piano* are reduced to victims of our human fascination with statistics and technology (p. 132).

"The novel's title comes from one of the first machines to replace human beings," notes Marvin (2002, p. 36). The player piano in the Homestead Bar serves as a central symbol that merges Vonnegut's themes of mechanization, art, and humanity. Readers and students can see that Vonnegut offers a tension between art and technology that is similar to Thoreau's contrast between technology and nature. Both Thoreau and Vonnegut argue in effect that technology can destroy the essential nature of being human. Marvin offers a number of points about the use of the player piano as a symbol in the novel:

- The player piano is historically significant as a way that humans recorded sound. Further, the "punch-card" aspect of the player piano parallels the punch-card information system used in the futuristic society of the novel. The format is now archaic by several generations, but at mid-twentieth century the punch card ran computers in much the same way the optical and disk drives do today. Marvin (2002) explains that the player piano produces music that pales in contrast to music played by a human just as the information cards do not adequately represent the humanity of people in the society (p. 37).
- When the player piano is playing, one character, Rudy, mentions that the playing appears to be done by a ghost (echoing the Ghost Shirt Society); Marvin believes that this reinforces Vonnegut's theme about technology and industrialization: "Of course, the machine has no heart, and mechanization has made ghosts of men who once had jobs and a sense of purpose in life. Their contributions to the industrial system are invisible, like the hands that play the piano" (p. 37). If students are reading and studying Thoreau and Vonnegut, they may be asked to compare and contrast Thoreau's belief that occupations create machines of humans with Vonnegut's assertion that the *loss* of occupations to machines has reduced humans to ghosts. We might also argue with

students that Thoreau and Vonnegut are not presenting contrasting views but nuanced arguments from a similar perspective.
- The irony of the player piano as symbol is that the pianos "are more versatile than other recording devices because they can also be played by a musician, just like a regular piano" (Marvin, 2002, p. 37). Marvin discusses that the player piano is a "symbol of the system" and that Finnerty playing an improvised tune "suggests that it is not too late for people to reclaim control of their lives" (pp. 37–38). The playing of the piano by Finnerty also emphasizes passion and emotion in human endeavors as a contrast to the purely intellectual focus of technology and mechanization.

The player piano as a central symbol is supported throughout by other brief symbolic moments that highlight the contrast between life and technology. Marvin (2002) notes the early scene when Paul asks for the cat to be taken to his office after the animal is killed by an automatic sweeper. Students can be asked to find similar supporting scenes in the novel as well as identifying these same conflicts in our real lives.

Galapagos—Evolution and the Teaching of Evolution

In reviewing *Galapagos,* Bianculli (Mustazza, 1994) states, "Vonnegut has crafted [the novel] . . . to present the evolution of the human race—as he imagines it will be—in the same methodical, complete, detached tones with which Darwin noted the evidence of evolution in the stranded creatures of the Galapagos Islands" (p. 276). Vonnegut has fictionalized one of the most influential and controversial of all scientific theories in his work from 1985. I doubt that Vonnegut would have imagined that twenty years after this novel, many states across the U.S. would be deeply embroiled in further arguments about teaching evolution in public school science classes. Once called "Creationism," a new argument against evolutionary science has raised its head, now repackaged as "Intelligent Design" and receiving direct endorsements by the president of the United States. Because of these developments, I will argue that there has never been a more important time to bring science fiction into our English classes (and into science classes) so our students are not unfairly propagandized by ideological arguments on both sides.

- -
CONNECTIONS

Many literary and scholarly works address the never-ending argument in America concerning the teaching of evolution in our schools. Students will enjoy the play and movie version of *Inherit the Wind* by Jerome Lawrence and Robert E. Lee. This modern classic dramatizes the infamous Monkey Trial of 1925 that highlighted the teaching of evolution by John Scopes in Tennessee. Clarence Darrow and William Jennings Bryan prove to be formidable historical figures and literary characters. The play changes names and some historical details but is essentially based in truth. For a wonderful historical account of the Scopes Trial, I recommend Edward J. Larson's *Summer for the Gods: The Scopes Trial and America's Continuing Debate over Science and Religion*. This excellent scholarly work helps clarify the details manipulated by the play; Larson's book also helps locate the larger debate between science and religion that continues to fester in America.

- -

While literature deserves to be read for its own sake, a work can also serve as one avenue to exploring a complex idea or debate more fully. I recommend that we use *Galapagos* to ask students to expand their understanding of evolutionary science and to provide them with both an awareness of and a perspective for the perpetual arguments that simmer and boil throughout America concerning the teaching of evolution in high school and college science courses. Let's look here briefly at how the novel can achieve both.

A first step for these goals is that we as teachers sharpen our own understanding of evolutionary science and the ongoing debates about teaching it. I highly recommend that English teachers work with teachers in the sciences, possibly team-teaching *Galapagos* as part of both English and science courses. Further, I recommend reading Howard Gardner's *The Disciplined Mind,* in which he discusses how we might use the teaching of evolutionary science as a central part of helping students to learn and think *as scientists do*. Scientific evidence and literary evidence have some qualities in common, but each discipline has unique conventions and expectations for scholarship and rigor as well. We need to sharpen our understanding of those commonalities and distinctions before asking the same of our students.

Next, we ask students to explore evolutionary science or the debates about teaching evolution or both. Evolutionary science requires students to examine the scientific method, the actual events surrounding Charles Darwin's initial theory of evolution, the history of how evolutionary theory has itself evolved, and the nature of terminology such as "theory" (it is common for students and most lay people to confuse a hypothesis with a theory, failing to recognize that in science a theory has been proven with evidence). Students could be divided into groups or asked individually to gather information about any or all of the areas to share with the entire class. The theory of evolution suffers from a great deal of urban legends and simple misinformation. Studying *Galapagos* can be an engaging opportunity for students to clarify and discount much of that information. One excellent initial source is a wonderful web page that allows students to explore the Galapagos Islands virtually (http://pubs.nsta.org/galapagos/). This web page is provided by the Smithsonian Institution and is supported by the National Science Foundation. While our English classes are not science classes, either alone or in conjunction with science teachers, we can ask students to use the theory of evolution as an opportunity to explain complex ideas clearly and fairly.

Further, we should offer students the opportunity to examine closely the evolution debate that has existed in American for about 80 years, if we consider the Scopes trials of 1925 as a starting point. I want to make one clarification: I support fully the teaching of evolutionary science in the appropriate science courses and reject Intelligent Design as a valid topic for science curriculum. However, I also support that in English courses, humanities courses, or interdisciplinary courses, students will benefit greatly from wrestling with identifying a broad spectrum of perspectives concerning the origin and development of humans. Students need to see why evolution creates such a firestorm of debate. In a science course, we cannot allow the perception of debates that do not exist; again, Intelligent Design is not a scientific argument, thus making it inappropriate for the science curriculum. But philosophical and religious arguments are equally as valid as scientific ones; in an English course we can offer students appropriate experiences that allow them to negotiate varying perspectives without corrupting any particular discipline. I think we have no desire to prejudice a scientific perspective over a religious one, but I do feel that we have an obligation to help students see the difference before they make commitments.

Studying *Galapagos* can lead to our students being able to explain more fully evolutionary science as well as being able to enter public discourse concerning the teaching of evolution as sophisticated contributors to that debate. I hope, with these goals in mind, that we do not allow the novel itself to be discounted as a work of art.

Galapagos—Vonnegut as Part of the American Literary Tradition

Galapagos also fits well into our curricular goals if we hope to share with students a sense of the American literary tradition: "Vonnegut may well be *the* representative American writer of the latter half of the twentieth century," argues Morse (2003, p. 1). Morse places

Vonnegut in a continuum that begins with Emerson and Thoreau. Let's look at how *Galapagos* captures the qualities we associate with American literature:

- Morse (2003) finds that Vonnegut captures his time period just as the great writers of American literature always have. From Emerson and Thoreau to Twain to Vonnegut, students can see in the great works by American writers how each generation has both enduring and unique qualities.
- Vonnegut's *Galapagos* also raises universal concerns. Thoreau, Twain, and Vonnegut share "a jaundiced eye on what his neighbors call 'progress'" (Morse, 2003, p. 2). Skepticism about technology and progress is not unique to science fiction but central to many of the great works in American letters.
- Vonnegut also exhibits a sense of social justice and action from that commitment that is found often in American works. "Vonnegut's ethically oriented fiction" asks readers to do something—again as Twain does, as Thoreau does (Morse, 2003, p. 2). Further, Morse quotes Richard Rorty to emphasize the importance of social justice in the work of Vonnegut as well as Americans as diverse as Walt Whitman and John Dewey (p. 3). Morse concludes, "Vonnegut is . . . no *spectator* but an *agent* for change" (p. 4).
- Vonnegut also shares with great American writers a relentless commitment to democracy and a fervent rejection of authoritarianism: "Vonnegut consistently and continually argues against authoritarianism and in favor of democracy, against military values and in favor of individual freedom, against imparting virtue to the accident of wealth and in favor of radically altering the conditions of the poor" (Morse, 2003, p. 4).
- Morse (2003) adds, "Emerson suggested that Americans belong either to the party of hope or the party of memory," concluding that Vonnegut "belongs to the party of hope" and that Vonnegut's "novels also reflect the party of hope's belief that individuals do make a difference" (p. 7). In *Galapagos,* Vonnegut, then, is dealing with not only the evolution of humanity but also the natural and inevitable change that typifies the American democratic experiment.

CONNECTION

Morse (2003) notes many major writers and thinkers in the American tradition—Emerson, Thoreau, Whitman, Dewey, Twain—suggesting Vonnegut's value as an American artist. If our courses seek to teach students aspects of that

American literary tradition, we can connect Emerson's "The American Scholar" with Vonnegut's *Galapagos*. Emerson offers a characterization of the American scholar. Students can first analyze Emerson's characterization from the nineteenth century; then they can compare that with both their perception of the American scholar and how Vonnegut's novel expresses Emerson's ideas and Vonnegut's own nuances. These considerations lead naturally to discussing what it means to be an American—as well as what it *should* mean to be an American. These are certainly relevant concerns for young people at the beginning of the twenty-first century.

Galapagos in some respects maintains many of the characteristics most associated with Vonnegut, but the novel moves beyond those characteristics. As a work of literary merit, *Galapagos* offers a valuable and vivid contribution to the American tradition.

Galapagos—Science Fiction and Myth

I have not intended to suggest that either *Player Piano* or *Galapagos* is unworthy of our classroom except as a vehicle to some other topic. I believe both are fine novels that deserve to be studied on their own merit. I agree with Mustazza (1990), actually, that *Galapagos* may be Vonnegut's "very best novel" or at least one of his very best (p. 166). According to Mustazza, "The brilliance of *Galapagos*, in fact, lies precisely in Vonnegut's deft fusion of future orientation—science fiction—and backward-looking narrative form—myth" (p. 167). I have already placed *Galapagos* in the dystopian tradition of science fiction; here I want to end this chapter discussing Vonnegut's use of the inverted Garden of Eden myth as a central motif of the novel.

The Garden of Eden myth casts the Tree of Knowledge as taboo. Humanity in Vonnegut's *Galapagos* has reverted to a state of intellectual innocence. The narrator points to the source of evil on the planet in much the same way as the narrative of Genesis does: "There was no other source [of evil]. This was a very innocent planet, except for those great big brains"—the storehouse of knowledge, of course (p. 9).

ENTRY POINT

While many myths included in Genesis are commonly recognized by students, students have rarely spent a great deal of time with the actual text of Genesis. Reading and rereading Genesis by students as an activity to clarify and outline the stories (often in multiple forms) will provide a solid foundation for identifying the Garden of Eden myth and other Genesis myths within *Galapagos*.

Mustazza (1990) looks at the Garden of Eden myth and the myth of the flood primarily in his critical consideration of Vonnegut's novel; therefore, we might want to limit what chapters of Genesis we ask students to analyze closely.

In our classrooms, this connection should address questions such as the following:

- What implication should readers draw from Vonnegut's connection between the human big brain and evil?
- How does Vonnegut's speculation about human evolution contrast with your view of humanity in the future?
- What does Vonnegut's narrative suggest about Social Darwinism?
- How does a writer's use of mythological archetypes contribute to the meaning of a literary work?
- What does this novel suggest about art, science, and religion?
- How is *Galapagos* a commentary on utopian societies?
- What does Vonnegut suggest here about concepts such as "innocence" and "evil"? What does the novel express about knowledge?

CONNECTIONS

William Blake devoted a great deal of his poetry to exploring the nature of innocence and experience. Combining his "The Lamb" and "The Tyger" with Billy Joel's "Only the Good Die Young" has proven to be an engaging and effective way to have students discuss the nature of innocence and experience.

- What does this novel capture about the dynamic between humanity and nature? Where does the ultimate power in the universe lie?

Vonnegut forces us as teachers, readers, and students to confront the big issues of existence. Although his stories and plots involve fantastic and somewhat overwhelming alternatives to this world, Vonnegut also never allows us to forget the face of *people,* particularly the humanity that is captured in those faces. Humans are frail and flawed and beautiful and dangerous. As a scholar himself, a scholar uniquely American, Vonnegut begs us to be like him—to confront these questions relentlessly in hopes that we will make the changes that cherish all that is good about being human.

ENTRY POINTS AND CONNECTIONS

The Metamorphosis, Franz Kafka

"The Scientist," Coldplay

"The Tables Turned," William Wordsworth

"since feeling is first," e. e. cummings

Planet of the Apes

Soylent Green

No Exit, Jean-Paul Sartre

The Mismeasure of Man, Stephen Jay Gould

The Case Against Standardized Testing, Alfie Kohn

The Hero with a Thousand Faces, Joseph Campbell

Zelig, Woody Allen, director

"Civil Disobedience" and *Walden,* Henry David Thoreau

Inherit the Wind, Jerome Lawrence and Robert E. Lee

Summer for the Gods: The Scopes Trial and America's Continuing Debate over Science and Religion, Edward J. Larson

"The American Scholar," Ralph Waldo Emerson

"The Lamb," "The Tyger," William Blake

"Only the Good Die Young," Billy Joel

Chapter Six

Bluebeard and Breakfast of Champions

Art, Pop Art, and American Culture

Throughout the discussions in this book, I have noted the themes and patterns we most commonly associate with Vonnegut, primarily his concern for science and technology along with his running debate over free will. But Vonnegut's writing clearly deals often with the broad issue of art and how art is portrayed and embraced (or not) in American society. *Bluebeard* and *Breakfast of Champions,* separately or as a paired novel unit, both confront the nature of art and the role of the artist in any society, though America's unique qualities are central in each novel. These novels also share the character Rabo Karabekian, who appears first in *Breakfast of Champions* and then resurfaces as the narrator of *Bluebeard*. Referring to *Bluebeard* as "the best of his later novels," Marvin (2002) notes, "Almost all of the novel's major characters are artists, and Vonnegut reflects on the importance of art to society and the individuals who create it" (p. 136). Schatt (1976) discusses that *Breakfast of Champions,* although less directly than *Bluebeard,* portrays Vonnegut's concern for art, Pop Art, and American commercialism; in this novel, much of that commentary grows from Vonnegut's own drawings: "Many of Vonnegut's drawings resemble work by . . . Pop artists" (p. 102). *Breakfast of Champions* is unique for Vonnegut's artwork that punctuates much of the text; that artwork is sparse and it often includes handwritten words—characteristics that many now associate with Vonnegut (and a style that has reached maturity in his latest book, *A Man without a Country,* in the form of aphorisms as graphic art).

In this chapter, I will explore how both novels can be brought into the high school or college English classroom as rich novel units on their own merits along with asking students to consider and reconsider art and the role of artists, particularly in American culture where utilitarian and financial qualities often trump artistic merit. These novels also raise issues about female characters in Vonnegut's fiction, the power of storytelling, the novel as a genre, popular culture and consumerism, and dark humor.

What Is Art?—The Role of Artists in the USA

"*Bluebeard* is first and foremost a book about artists and the role of art in contemporary American society," Marvin (2002) explains, adding that the novel "affirms the fundamental human need to play and create" (p. 149). Vonnegut himself and the characters he creates embody that argument for the power of and need for art, for creativity in the human condition. While the English classroom is ripe for exploring creativity and experiencing creativity, I am skeptical that many students associate their English classes with opportunities to explore their creativity; in fact, I am suspicious that our students often see English class (and most any class) as simply filling some adults' requirements and expectations, the antithesis of creativity. In his discussion, "Vonnegut and Aesthetic Humanism," Andrews (Boon, 2001) concludes that Vonnegut views art as "a communal activity designed to increase human kindness, thus answering the answerable question, 'what are the arts for?'"—a question the novel poses for our students (p. 41).

ENTRY POINTS

Many works of literature directly confront the essential nature of art and the role of the artist in the creation of that art. John Keats's "Ode on a Grecian Urn" and Marge Piercy's "A Work of Artifice" give readers two images of art through the urn (and the artwork on that urn) and the bonsai tree. The urn as a human-created object and the bonsai tree as a human-manipulated object both represent artwork, and students can be asked what makes each art. Further, we can ask students to discuss how the poems are similar in their portrayals of art and how they are different. Keats has a Romantic agenda in his poem, arguing for the immutable nature of art as the human attempt at immortality; Piercy's poem begins with art and ends with a feminist slant. The tones of these poems contrast because of the broader themes that grow from the art theme in each. These poems can initiate for students their own perceptions of art and being artistic as they begin reading and discussing Vonnegut's novels.

In the "Author's Note" to *Bluebeard,* Vonnegut explains that his novel is a "hoax autobiography" of artist Rabo Karabekian, emphasizing that readers should not view the novel as "a responsible history of the Abstract Expressionist school of painting" in America (p. i). However, this note ends with a clear message that Vonnegut himself is skeptical of the negative impact wealth has had on the American perception of art, ending his note with his own view that "children's games" are art as well (p. i). Andrews (Boon, 2001) argues that "what Vonnegut and *Bluebeard* do best is dissect the various historical processes that corrupt art" (p. 19). *Bluebeard* is Vonnegut's art novel since the characters and the plot both focus primarily on the lives of artists. One way to have students consider the art themes in the novel is to have them explore the variety of artists portrayed by the characters; let's look at those characters briefly here:

- Rabo Karabekian—The first-person narrator of this fictional autobiography (similar to Vonnegut's *Mother Night*). Marvin (2002) recognizes that Karabekian's personality tends to emulate those around him as does his development as an artist. Karabekian becomes an artist directly through the influence of Dan Gregory and indirectly through the influence of Jackson Pollock (the personification of the Abstract Expressionism movement in America and the primary real-world artist in the novel). Karabekian returns from World War II and "falls under the sway of a poor role model, the alcoholic painter, Terry Kitchen" (Marvin, 2002, p. 145). Kitchen commits suicide (alluding to the debate over Pollock's death), and Karabekian, whose life has already begun to crumble, becomes a recluse. His life as an artist is punctuated by having painted with Sateen Dura Luxe, which eventually crumbles off his canvasses, and by completing one final giant painting that remains hidden from others and the reader until the end of the novel. Karabekian's art and development as an artist provide students with a number of angles from which to argue the nature of art and the role of the artist.

CONNECTION

Vonnegut includes Jackson Pollock in his novel, connecting this work of fiction with the real-world debate over art that Pollock himself embodied. The independent movie biography of the artist, *Pollock,* stars Ed Harris, who also directed. This movie can serve as a valuable connection for students, particularly if they have little or no knowledge of the debates that often remain vibrant within art communities. The artist Jackson Pollock stood in the middle of that debate over Abstract Expressionism, which forced artists and laypeople alike to debate the nature of art and the role of the artist. The turbulent and brief life of Pollock also allows us to discuss with students some of the stereotypes perpetuated about artists; Pollock did struggle with substance abuse, and he did die mysteriously, leading some to suggest suicide. Yet, his life and art ask students to define art and to reconsider who artists are—as artists and people. Paired with *Bluebeard*, this movie may give context to the themes Vonnegut explores in the novel.

- Edith Taft Fairbanks—His sole happy relationship seems to be his marriage to Edith, his surrogate mother (Marvin, 2002). Her character contributes to the art motif through her symbolic motherhood, which is literally a creative act. Her role is complex in that her affection and nurturing qualities contrast Karabekian's "failure to look beyond the surface appearance of things" (Marvin, p. 146). This contrast emphasizes Karabekian's physical limitations (only one good eye) as representations of his artistic and personal failures.
- Circe Berman—"A Judy Blume-type writer" (Boon, 2001, p. 24), Berman serves two artistic purposes in the novel. Her allusive name places her within the *Odyssey* motif of the novel—along with the image of Karabekian as a Cyclops—and her role as a successful writer of adolescent literature contributes to the tensions in the novel between art for art's sake and art for profit. Berman's realistic work written for adolescents provokes one of the debates about art that is most relevant to high school and college students, who have a central part in the debate over the appropriate novels they should be asked to read in school. Having students research and debate the endless argument over the literary canon and take a stand on the value of adolescent literature are valuable experiences as those students develop their own sense of art.
- Paul Slazinger—Something of a contrast with Berman at first, Slazinger is a serious novelist who detests Berman initially and who "suffers from writer's block" (Marvin, 2002, p. 137). Andrews (Boon, 2001) suggests that the "true if subtle villain of *Bluebeard* is 'serious'" (p. 26). Slazinger suffers for his art in a dramatic way that Vonnegut seems to reject much in the same way he rejects all of the extremes in the novel, extremes that appear to have only a corrupting effect on art—art, which should be a "celebration" according to Andrews, who quotes John Dewey (Boon, p. 26). Slazinger ultimately reassesses the work of Berman at the end of the novel (when the setting returns to the 1987 "present" of the work) and ironically dedicates himself to establishing Berman's work as high literature and to securing her novels' rightful place among the canon; Slazinger also begins writing non-

fiction, another interesting twist in the debate over quality literature (Is serious literature only fiction?).

- Dan Gregory—Andrews (Boon, 2001) characterizes Gregory as "a commercial artist whose sentimentality and popularity recall Norman Rockwell" (p. 20). Gregory serves as Karabekian's first artistic mentor, and students should be asked to consider the nature of commercial and popular art through Gregory. Works by Rockwell can be points of contention concerning the nature of art much in the same way as the works of Pollock are. The Gregory/Rockwell focus concerns commercial art, a utilitarian and popular intent for creativity. Artistic Realism is also addressed through Gregory—a movement in the visual arts that stands in stark contrast to Abstract Expressionism.
- Terry Kitchen—The fictional parallel to Pollock, Kitchen personifies Vonnegut's interesting skepticism of and "admiration for the paintings of Pollock and Kitchen," which Andrews (Boon, 2001) explains "is consistent with [Vonnegut's] interest in artistic revolutionaries such as Matisse, Picasso, Braque, Klee, and others, all of whom manipulate relatively abstract techniques to expressive ends" (pp. 20–21). Kitchen and Gregory combine as characters and as representations of artistic purposes to reveal Vonnegut's belief, according to Andrews, that "[t]aken to extremes, mimesis [Gregory] and abstraction [Kitchen] thus become equally formalistic, equally inhuman" (p. 21).
- Marilee Kemp—The mistress of Gregory, Kemp is Karabekian's first sexual experience (thus creative), and she serves as one of the writers in the novel who expands the themes about art and creativity beyond the visual arts. Kemp "discovers her talent for writing in her letters to Karabekian" (Marvin, 2002, p. 148) and begins to find her own voice, thus empowerment, through expression, through art (a theme I will explore more fully in a later section). While other characters are associated with movements in the visual arts, Kemp serves as a focal point for how art serves individuals and society, notably those with no voice, with no power.

"Vonnegut often distinguishes between authors who respond directly to life and those who respond to life by way of art history," explains Andrews (Boon, 2001, p. 39). The novel, students should come to see, places a premium on responding to life, thus creating art, and on "communal expression," Andrews notes, as a way for humans to share our humanity (p. 39). This novel offers a wealth of opportunities for students to argue the nature of art and the role of artists. Vonnegut's work makes some clear claims on those topics, but it shares enough ambiguity about the debates to make this novel ideal for our classrooms, where we wish to raise more questions than we hope to answer.

Vonnegut's Female Characters—Feminism and the Vonnegut Canon

"Feminist critics would find little to praise and much to condemn in Vonnegut's earlier novels," admits Marvin (2002), but he adds that *Bluebeard* overcomes that weakness (p. 154). As my brief detailing of the artistic characters above suggests, several fully developed and significant women populate this novel. The themes and motifs dealing with art often intertwine with considerations about the dynamics between men and women along with the essential struggle women face concerning their own empowerment in societies still dominated in many ways by men. I see Vonnegut's concern for art illuminating his exploration of more fully developed female characters since he sees art as an empowering experience for the artist and that artist's audiences.

To frame Vonnegut's feminist themes, let's begin with the end of the novel when Karabekian finally explains his long-hidden giant painting to Circe Berman. Karabekian's masterpiece is eight feet high and sixty-four feet long; it is highly detailed as well, overwhelming any viewer. Here we will focus on Karabekian and Berman's discussion of the portrayal of women in the painting before moving on to some of the female characters in the novel and how they contribute to Vonnegut's work as a whole. At first, Circe sees no women in the painting. After Karabekian urges her to look closer, she makes yet another mistake: "There don't seem to be any *healthy* women" (p. 302). But Karabekian corrects her; the healthy women are hiding in the cellar attempting to avoid being raped—"[T]hey have heard the history of other wars in the area, so they know that rape will surely come," explains Karabekian (p. 303). These symbolic elements in the painting are powerful, especially at the end of the novel, testaments to Vonnegut's messages as a novelist, but he doesn't stop there. Karabekian tells Circe that the painting is titled "Now It's the Women's Turn" (p. 303).

Karabekian's giant painting pulls together motifs that Vonnegut dramatizes in the novel. The role of women in society is clearly addressed, but more directly, the painting and Vonnegut highlight that women suffer in horrifying and unique ways due to wars, which are primarily the result of decisions made by men. Those horrors include sexual abuse, such as rape, and sexual manipulations that are not as overt as rape. Karabekian is careful to tell Circe that half of the unhealthy people in the painting are women, suggesting some level of shared suffering between men and women. Yet, it appears to be *only* women in the cellar hiding from the rape that is an unavoidable partner with war. While the painting itself captures a great deal of horror and even hopelessness, I feel that the novel overall has a much more optimistic message that is directly related to the power of art. Marvin (2002) ends his discussion of the novel with, "*Bluebeard* shows that from a woman's point of view, war is the ultimate form of male aggression against women and until women are in a position of power, there is little hope for a better world" (p. 156). How can women gain that power? I see the answer in Vonnegut's novel—through the power of language and the power of art.

Marilee Kemp and Circe Berman rise above other female characters in Vonnegut's works who appear more often than not to be symbolic elements in the story instead of three-dimensional characters. Marilee could have easily been yet another sexual toy for a Vonnegut male character; his works have memorable female characters who fit that description. But she is much more than the physically abused lover of Dan Gregory and Count Bruno Portomaggiore. Marvin (2002) recognizes that Vonnegut "rewrites the Cinderella story so that Marilee saves herself" (p. 155). The key to this transformation and Marilee's ability to enact it herself is the power of language as art: "Becoming a writer transforms her from an object to a subject . . . , but only after [the Count's] death is Marilee free to write her own happy ending to her amazing story" (Marvin, p. 156). She becomes a highly successful businessperson after being freed from a man who hoarded homosexual pornography and is "laughed at [for] his cowardice and vanity and effeminacy" (p. 244). Some of Vonnegut's purposes with Marilee's character and life must include gender roles since Marilee acquires traditionally male characteristics while the Count suffers for and hides feminine qualities.

CONNECTION

The feminist movement and feminist ideology have suffered from both deserved and exaggerated claims that feminism is simply organized male bashing. Modern female novelists such as Margaret Atwood have taken complex stances in their literature that are skeptical of extreme feminist positions while also criticizing the negative results of patriarchal societies and assumptions of male superiority. One element that is repeated in feminist motifs is the oppressive nature of marriage (or committed relationships) for women. Kate Chopin's "The Story of an Hour" parallels Marilee's Cinderella motif in the novel, except that Mrs. Mallard in Chopin's story experiences only a brief earthly freedom followed by death, a sort of freedom but one not as optimistic as Marilee's success after the

Count's death. Pairing the Chopin story with Marilee's story can force students to discuss the nature of marriage, the ability of women to be empowered, and the role art and language play in those dynamics. (Does the fact that Marilee has a life as a writer benefit her in ways that are not available to Mrs. Mallard?)

- -

Marvin (2002) identifies Circe Berman as a uniquely "well-developed character in her own right" who is able to explain to Karabekian Marilee's empowerment; Circe recognizes (and probably echoes Vonnegut's belief) that writers need an audience to grow even if it is "an audience of *one*" (p. 65). Berman and Karabekian continue to discuss the importance of an audience, which leads Berman to confess that her audience is her dead husband, a technique she believes is the secret to her success. Like Marilee, Circe has a deceased husband, but in contrast to Marilee's situation, Circe's husband appears to be an ideal, a source of inspiration—an inversion of the traditional use of women as inspiration. Many critics note that Karabekian experiences a series of flawed mentors in his life, but we might argue that his best mentor is Berman, who has the confidence in her own art that Karabekian never experiences. As well, Circe contrasts Marilee in that her "aid is asexual," states Andrews (Boon, 2001, p. 40). Her mentoring role could be described as both mother and father without the usual Oedipal elements we tend to anticipate.

If we return to the end of the novel, where I began this section, let's recall that the unveiling of Karabekian's final artwork and the subsequent explanation of that painting are shared with Berman, suggesting that the painting becomes some message he must share with an audience, ironically an audience of one that has been championed by Circe herself. I am not inclined to categorize Vonnegut as a sexist author, either intentionally or through some flaw in his sensitivity to women, but I do acknowledge that *Bluebeard* addresses the plight of women and the value of language for women well, probably more effectively than in any other work by Vonnegut. I would add, however, that I can find many positive messages about women—and about all humanity—throughout Vonnegut's works. That humans need to love each other is certainly a theme feminists are eager to embrace even when a work of literature includes Montana Wildhack.

Stories and Journeys—Empowerment and a Homeric Motif

Maxine Greene (1995) offers:

> As a set of techniques, literacy has often silenced persons and disempowered them. Our obligation today is to find ways of enabling

the young to find their voices, to open their spaces, to reclaim their histories in their variety and discontinuity. (p. 120)

Like Freire (1993) and Vonnegut, Greene sees literacy and expression through art as central elements of what we share with students in our schools if our goal is individual empowerment. In *Bluebeard,* Vonnegut shows this journey through the character of Marilee, and he also shows the journey motif in his use of Homeric motifs throughout the novel: "The master theme of both *Bluebeard* and *The Odyssey* is the longing for community," explains Andrews (Boon, 2001, p. 39). In this section, I want to explore how literacy, art, and community are combined in Vonnegut's novel and how these motifs contribute to the growth and empowerment of our English students.

Storytelling can be seen as a type of journey. The many versions of storytelling in *Bluebeard* parallel and reinforce the Homeric motifs that Vonnegut weaves throughout the novel. For our students, we can discuss the power of storytelling—"to open their spaces, to reclaim their histories," as Greene (1995, p. 120) states—in their lives as we detail that same power in the lives of the characters. Marilee, as I highlighted above, finds her empowerment in her writing for an audience of one; further, once empowered by the death of the count, she writes her own future, personifying Greene's ideas about finding one's voice. Circe is also a storyteller; her storytelling is written for an audience of one, her deceased and idealized husband, but shared with adolescents primarily and adults as well—an audience that appears to need the connection she provides. The serious novelist Slazinger is interesting in that he appears to find his voice after his career is interrupted by writer's block, and he reinvents himself by beginning a work of nonfiction. Here, we have an opportunity to discuss the values of fiction and nonfiction with our students. In Vonnegut's own career, he seems to have turned more and more from pure fiction toward a nonfiction-like fiction and finally to pure nonfiction with his most recent published writings.

CONNECTION

Marilee and Karabekian have a heated argument about Henrik Ibsen's *A Doll's House.* Marilee is furious that Nora leaves her home and family and believes that the "'ending is *fake!*'" (p. 159). She feels an honest ending would have been Nora's suicide. This play parallels Marilee's own existence with Gregory, according to Karabekian. Students should be confronted with Marilee's complaint in order to debate it themselves. If they have read Chopin's "A Story of an Hour" in connection with Marilee's characterization in *Bluebeard,* they can continue by discussing how literature portrays marriage as a prison for women and how literature characterizes women's freedom from those prisons. This section of the novel ends with Karabekian sharing that Marilee offers one more comment about the play: "'She should have stayed home and made the best of things'" (p. 160). Marilee seems confused and ultimately upset that the play ignores the journey that lies ahead for Nora while Karabekian remains focused on how the play parallels Marilee's life.

The writers in the novel, however, are not the only storytellers. The visual artists are storytellers also. Two elements of visual art as storytelling, as finding one's voice, are worth pursuing with our students. First, Karabekian's final giant painting is clearly a visual representation of a story. His career is punctuated with starkly realistic representations of the world and with Abstract Expressionism, leading to the second aspect of visual art as storytelling—Does abstract artwork tell a story? Does abstract artwork say *anything*? Vonnegut appears to be addressing these concerns, and his exploration gains complexity and authenticity because of his own pursuits as a writer and as a visual artist.

Vonnegut offers his reader a storytelling filled with storytelling. As well, Vonnegut has created an ambiguous work that appears simultaneously to refute and practice traditional techniques of storytelling and authoritarian guidelines for judging art: "The best example of this strategy may be the novel's Homeric motifs, which suggest that *Bluebeard* is as obsessed with literary history as it is with art history," Andrews (Boon, 2001, p. 39) argues. I believe Vonnegut and Greene have a similar concern that traditional expectations and authoritarian structures have the tendency to use literacy as a silencing and controlling force instead of part of a journey toward empowerment and self-actualization. Andrews accurately notes that Vonnegut practices Modernist techniques—weaving allusions and motifs from *The Odyssey* throughout the novel, for example—in order to confront the dangers he perceives in those traditions.

Vonnegut's works always reflect his training as an anthropologist (Marvin, 2002; Boon, 2001), and *Bluebeard* uses motifs from *The Odyssey* to express his recurring concern for community; the journey motif shows the human need to find the Self and to discover one's community, and the storytelling motif emphasizes the human need to communicate—without an audience, what purpose the author? In typical Vonnegut fashion, however, the novel moves beyond these classic motifs and manipulates them. Some of the Homeric elements in the novel include:

- Rabo Karabekian embodies conflicting forces in *The Odyssey* concerning community. Karabekian is portrayed as Polyphemus, the Cyclops: "Vonnegut makes Rabo one-eyed and has him refer to himself as a 'Cyclops' and a 'hermit' so as to refer to that force in his character that inclines toward Cyclopean isolation—and to label that characteristic essentially negative," explains Andrews (Boon, 2001, p. 39). Concurrently, the novel shows the story of a journey since Karabekian is, of course, seeking home and community throughout his memoir, although he tends to do so badly. The irony of Vonnegut's use of Odysseus's journey is that the reader follows the journey of the Cyclops and not Odysseus, the journey of the hermit, not the hero.
- Vonnegut's ironic twist on Homeric motifs continues with Circe Berman: "Circe, a bewitching guest, forces Rabo to stop being the pig he has long been," explains Andrews (Boon, 2001, p. 40). Circe in *The Odyssey* lures men into her trap, turning them into swine with her sexual allure. In *Bluebeard,* as noted earlier, Circe is "asexual" (Boon, p. 40), and her power over Rabo is positive and engaging.
- Andrews (Boon, 2001) also identifies a Homeric motif in the relationship between Rabo and his housekeeper-cook's daughter, Celeste. Again, this pattern from *The Odyssey* has a twist. Celeste is chastised by Karabekian for being ignorant of classic literature and high art, but she turns out to be expert in the works of Circe Berman, who Slazinger calls "'the Homer of the bubblegum crowd'" (p. 208). Andrews explains that Celeste "knows more about Homer than Rabo does" since Karabekian "seems to value . . . an empty knowledge, a knowledge for knowledge's sake that only deepens his isolation" (p. 40).

Possibly the pivotal story and moment in the many journeys of *Bluebeard* can be found near the middle of the book: "Circe Berman has just asked me how to tell a good picture from a bad one" (p. 165). This is the essential question of the book that Vonnegut manipulates in a variety of ways. Karabekian embraces an answer offered to him by Syd Solomon: "'All you have to do, my dear,' he said, 'is look at a million paintings, and then you can never be mistaken'" (p. 165). And this may be the solution for us as teachers if we attempt to fulfill Greene's charge; our students deserve millions of experiences with art, with literature, and with their lives. Such is the journey of their empowerment.

Of Novels and Anti-Novels

"And now comes the spiritual climax of this book, for it is at this point that I, the author, am suddenly transformed by what I have done so far," announces the narrator of *Breakfast of Champions,* the novel where Rabo Karabekian first appears and where Vonnegut deals with art and storytelling within the context of his broader satire of American culture (p. 224). While critics and Vonnegut himself often declare this novel something of a failure, many Vonnegut fans, myself included, treasure the work, and students often commit to Vonnegut because of this work, not *Slaughterhouse-Five*. Again like *Bluebeard, Breakfast of Champions* deals simultaneously with how humans define themselves and with the weight of suicide. First, let's look at the narrative techniques of this novel itself as one avenue to address Vonnegut's themes on art and language—and American culture.

"In many ways *Breakfast of Champions* is an anti-novel, a reaction to the fictional theories of Henry James that have dominated American fiction for almost a century," states Schatt (1976, p. 98). Vonnegut has explained that this novel once was a part of his *Slaughterhouse-Five,* another novel that can be called experimental. As an anti-novel, *Breakfast of Champions* allows students to explore and reconsider traditional elements of the novel and of fiction in general. Some of the experimental elements of this novel include the following:

- Schatt (1976) notes that Vonnegut "has always disliked the artificiality of the old-fashioned ending that neatly ties together everything and everybody" (p. 99). Further, Schatt adds that Vonnegut rejects "the conventional plot" and the clearly defined good and bad characters who receive neat "rewards" and "punishments" (p. 99). Therefore, *Breakfast of Champions* can serve as a discussion of plot and characterization in terms of traditional expectations (primarily supported by New Critical parameters) and the effectiveness of Vonnegut's manipulation of these techniques and expectations.
- The narration of the novel is also both experimental and a confrontation of conventional expectations: the reader forgets that she is reading and forgets that the work is fictional. In Chapter 18, the narrator confesses to being Vonnegut himself, who is essentially spying on his own characters, Dwayne Hoover and Kilgore Trout. This novel allows students to discuss the value of the narrator and the importance of the "vivid and continuous dream" endorsed by Gardner (1999, 1991).

"This was the reason Americans shot each other so often: It was a convenient literary device for ending short stories and books," Vonnegut explains as the narrator (p. 215). Vonnegut appears to be wrestling in *Breakfast of Champions* with the impact of art on culture as much as the impact of any culture—but specifically American culture—on art. In this novel, he declares, "I resolved to shun storytelling" and plans to set his characters free. The result is a novel that defies being a novel, making *Breakfast of Champions* more than Vonnegut musing about art; it is an opportunity for readers to contemplate the value of art and the conventional expectations of the novel.

An additional experimental quality of *Breakfast of Champions* is Vonnegut's use of his own unique artwork, sparse drawings of everything from a woman's genitalia to a simple rendition of three pyramids. This somewhat crude use of graphic art and writing have become synonymous with Vonnegut since he now sells his own artwork and uses as his signature piece his drawing of an anus from this novel (p. 5)—though he tends to refer to it as his asterisk.

CONNECTION

The graphic novel and its cousin the comic book are experiencing a renaissance today, although the comic book has been an underground source of literacy, particularly for male adolescents, for decades. *Breakfast of Champions* itself raises the issue of the value of Pop Art. Frank Miller, a comics writer and illustrator of some critical acclaim, has eventually brought his comic *Sin City* to the movie screen. His work can be found with classics such as Batman comics as well. Bringing graphic novels and comics into the classroom with *Breakfast of Champions* offers students an opportunity to explore Pop Art within the uniquely adolescent culture in a way that is absent in *Bluebeard*, which faces those arguments about art at a much different level.

Since the publication of this novel, iconography has mushroomed in contemporary culture in ways that *Breakfast of Champions* seems to foresee. The use of icons in computer software—and even in cell phones and iPods—has become a literacy skill all its own. E-mail and Instant Message shortcuts have also introduced icon literacy that replaces written words. Vonnegut confronts the reader with these very issues in this novel written (and drawn) in 1973.

Warning: This Novel Is Explicit

Bringing any new piece of literature into an English classroom can be a daunting experience. First, as teachers, we are concerned about our own level of expertise with a work before we attempt to teach it. Second, we are concerned about how students will respond to the work. And, broadly, we are sensitive to whether the work is appropriate for our students, both in terms of the maturity and in terms of how well it meets our instructional goals. *Breakfast of Champions* might be one of the most challenging works any teacher brings into a classroom.

Yes, this work is explicit, explicit in ways that gives the most open-minded of us pause. Vonnegut includes drawings of genitalia, repeated harsh profanity, sporadic detailing of penis lengths and women's measurements, and a casual use of a racial slur that seems beyond unnerving. If a work has a potential for being challenged in the classroom, *Breakfast of Champions* might be the champion of that category. Then why am I including it in this volume? Why am I suggesting that we teach this novel?

I would argue that Vonnegut's novel achieves something few works of art can claim; it shakes the reader throughout, and it forces every reader to rethink almost everything. To me that is the highest achievement of art. Vonnegut's approach is never direct and his message is never simplistic. I want to end this chapter on art and particularly the role of art and artists in American culture by listing many of the adept and humorous observations made by Vonnegut in this, my favorite and most often read Vonnegut novel:

- In the Preface, Vonnegut introduces the reader to the woman who used humor and bawdiness to teach him to be a skeptical learner, setting the stage for his own technique throughout the novel (which may be an extended tribute to Phoebe Hurty).
- Vonnegut argues throughout the novel that humans are robots, a realization that prods him to free his own characters. Thoreau makes this same argument in "Civil Disobedience" concerning the Mexican War. This is another discussion by Vonnegut about the nature of free will in humans. *Breakfast of Champions* fits perfectly in English classrooms filled with high school and college students who themselves are facing the adult world and discovering how free (or not) they are.
- Chapter 1 directly confronts American mythology, much as Howard Zinn does in *People's History of the United States*. How true are our stories of our nation? Vonnegut appears to ask his readers this question while weaving a story himself.
- Explicit drawings, explicit language, and racial slurs punctuate this entire novel. The explicit and offensive drawings and language seem to carry a detached tone by Vonnegut that intensifies their impact. Why does Vonnegut do this? While I believe students need to ask and answer this question on their own, I will add that the explicit elements of the novel combined with the detached tone are some aspects of the genius captured in this novel.

- Related to the explicit nature of the novel is Vonnegut's thematic interest in three major issues facing American culture: sexism, racism, and sexual squeamishness. Vonnegut as narrator maintains a matter-of-fact tone throughout the novel, particularly as he details the measurements of his female characters (playing off the 36–24–36 ideal of mid-century America), as he uses racial slurs in his narration (not just in the dialogue of racist characters), and as he describes the pornographic magazines where Kilgore Trout's writings are published. Readers must reevaluate the norms and conventions that Vonnegut exposes without any direct commentary. John Gardner argued in his theories of fiction that novels must be moral, but he (as does Vonnegut) realizes that preaching is not storytelling; thus, Vonnegut simply opens our eyes and shows us the worst he can imagine, trusting throughout that we will come to moral conclusions. In one of Trout's novels, "The humanoids wished they could put them [pornographic movie houses] out of business somehow, but without interfering with free speech" (p. 59). Much the same could be said about *Breakfast of Champions* or the ever-growing Internet in twenty-first century America.
- Vonnegut lets nothing go unscathed; the novel addresses religion, industry, politics, and consumerism. Again, he approaches these themes with a detached tone and through both his words and his art. In Chapter 8, he quickly associates a prostitute surrendering her free will to a pimp with her "surrender[ing herself] to Jesus" (p. 74). His attacks on all things sacred are quick and biting, revealing his own view of these issues while respecting the intellect of his readers.
- Again, through the stories attributed to Trout , Vonnegut looks at the arbitrary nature of judging art. In Chapter 14, a cab driver tells Trout he has read Trout's story about a "'government [that] used a kind of roulette wheel to decide what to put in the museums, and what to throw out'" (p. 132). The cab driver, ironically, is recalling having read that story while also using the story's pages as toilet paper.
- A scene that certainly belongs in every English classroom concerns Patty Keene, a waitress hoping to seduce Dwayne Hoover. When she apologizes to Hoover, the narrator adds, "She was used to apologizing for her use of language." Why? "She had been encouraged to do a lot of that in school." Who created this dynamic? "This was because their English teachers would wince and cover their ears and give them flunking grades and so on whenever they failed to speak like English aristocrats before the First World War" (p. 142). Vonnegut's sharp wit leaves not even the English teacher

- unscathed—and rightly so. We and our students would certainly benefit from discussing Vonnegut's characterization of English classes and English teachers.
- Issues of empowerment and oppression are woven throughout this novel. Patty says little to avoid sounding dumb, but she also remains silent about her being raped. Silence is a motif of the novel—one of the most horrifying motifs. What is said in America? "It didn't matter much what most people in Midland City said out loud, except when they were talking about money or structures or travel or machinery—or other measurable things" (p. 146). Within three pages, Vonnegut reveals that Patty remains silent about rape, but that what Americans say about "measurable things" (notably money) does matter. Few brief commentaries on America are more precise than this brief moment in Vonnegut's novel.
- "He was a graduate of West Point, a military academy which turned young men into homicidal maniacs for use in war"—again, Vonnegut addresses war in this novel (p. 157). The technique in *Breakfast of Champions* is distinct from *Slaughterhouse-Five*, novels separated by only four years (publication dates). In the latter work, Vonnegut already seems much more weary and pessimistic, seemingly brought down by the weight of the Vietnam years. Nonetheless, he speaks once again for a human need to seek peace, to regain our essential human nature.
- "Bunny Hoover, Dwayne's homosexual son," suffers a beating by his own father in the novel (p. 181). Contemporary students may have lived in an American society that has progressed in some ways concerning sexism and racism (although that assertion is debatable), but they have also witnessed a rise in homophobia and a greatly intensified cultural war about gay rights, specifically gay marriage. High school and college students of today see gay characters in popular culture regularly, on TV and in the movies. But the last twenty-five years have seen a cultural backlash against homosexuality as well, with many states voting to outlaw gay marriage and many pushing for a Constitutional amendment to ban such.
- "Much of the conversation in the country consisted of lines from television shows, both present and past"—and Vonnegut's observation from over thirty years ago can only be multiplied exponentially today (p. 236). The single most powerful aspect of popular culture in Americas is TV—even with the rise of cable networks dwarfing over-the-air networks and even with the Internet explosion. But what does Vonnegut say about the impact of TV in this novel? I am not certain we should use Vonnegut to

mindlessly bash popular culture or TV (respected writers such as Barbara Kingsolver, however, are quick to reject TV), but I do believe he wishes for his readers to *consider* the impact of TV on our daily lives, particularly concerning how we interact as humans.

Breakfast of Champions and *Bluebeard* are wonderful works of art that give life to the larger debates about art. In America, young people are far more likely to be familiar with the cereal slogan "Breakfast of Champions" (although in a newer form) than with Jackson Pollock. And we may find that fact sad. Vonnegut, however, doesn't seek to encourage elitist reactions by his readers. His works are not trashing popular culture and endorsing conventional views of High Art. Vonnegut questions *everything*. He doesn't offer anything certain or clear for readers, although he takes some firm stands on war, politics, consumerism, and the good ol' U.S. of A. *Breakfast of Champions* ends with a self-portrait of Vonnegut crying, and we are left asking ourselves what he is crying about. *That* act of wonderment by the reader/viewer is what art is all about.

ENTRY POINTS AND CONNECTIONS

"Ode on a Grecian Urn," John Keats

"A Work of Artifice," Marge Piercy

Pollock, Ed Harris, director

"The Story of an Hour," Kate Chopin

A Doll's House, Henrik Ibsen

Sin City, Frank Miller

Chapter Seven

Welcome to the Monkey House

Short Stories

"Thanks to popular magazines, I learned on the job to be a fiction writer," confesses Vonnegut (1999a) in his collection *Bagombo Snuff Box* (p. 290). Vonnegut began publishing in the latter part of the heyday in America for writers of short stories. J. D. Salinger, F. Scott Fitzgerald, and Ernest Hemingway all benefited from the possibility of earning a notable salary from publishing short fiction in the first half of the twentieth century. Vonnegut notes, however, "that it is no longer possible to make a living writing short stories" (p. 290). The study of short stories in our English classes has not diminished despite the fate suffered by those who pursue the craft. For me as an English teacher, Vonnegut saved my short story unit. Along with discussing using Vonnegut's short stories in our classes, I want to explore in this chapter how students can work on the craft of short story writing as they learn how to determine the quality of short stories.

Although Vonnegut earned enough money to commit his career to writing—even quitting his job with GE—Karon (Boon, 2001) explains, "No one prefers to speak about Kurt Vonnegut's short stories, and critics have often, without apology, denigrated them, particularly those stories from Vonnegut's early 'slick' submission period" (p. 105). Karon notes that many critics are now re-evaluating Vonnegut's short fiction more favorably—making his stories ideal for discussing popular and critical analyses of short stories. Asking students to immerse themselves more fully in collections of short stories raised my short story unit to a much higher level of engagement for my students. Vonnegut's *Welcome to the Monkey House* has always worked well as one of the collections students choose to read. Now let's look at Vonnegut's stories as valuable additions to our units dealing with short fiction as a genre and as a central aspect of American literature.

Examining and Evaluating the Short Story

Karon (Boon, 2001) and Vonnegut (2005) himself—one a critic, the other an author who values the form—offer students a number of avenues for judging the quality of short fiction. Somewhere so far in the past of my teaching that I can no longer cite the appropriate source of the idea, I began explaining to students that the short story is more like a poem than a novel. For teaching and learning, the short story is an excellent form for helping students develop their sense of literary analysis and their sense of what separates high art from popular art. In this section, I will discuss using Vonnegut's short stories as a part of a short story unit that explores the genre and will end this section by examining how Karon and Vonnegut analyze and evaluate short stories.

ENTRY POINT

By high school and college English courses, students have some clear expectations about short stories since short fiction is one of the most commonly studied genres in school. Most students have learned to some degree the terminology associated with the plot—exposition, complication, climax, and denouement (or some version of this pattern)—and with conflict—such as human versus human or human versus nature—so I have found that beginning a short story unit with a story that conflicts with any of those basic assumptions allows us as teachers to re-frame how students approach the form. William Carlos Williams's "The Use of Force" has always worked well as an entry point for discussing short stories for my classes. It is a brief story that fits traditional expectation about the form in some aspects while disorienting student readers with its abrupt ending, offering students an implied resolution instead of a neat and obvious ending (which they have studied in classes and experienced in popular forms of stories found in print and in video formats).

The short story unit in my American literature course eventually developed into the form I will outline briefly here. Vonnegut became a significant part of this unit in both his story "Harrison Bergeron" as a whole-class story to study and discuss and his collection *Welcome to the Monkey House*. I tended to work through this process in my short story unit to introduce students to the short story as a unique American form and to help them develop their analytical skills:

- The short story is often attributed in its modern form to Edgar Allan Poe and Nathaniel Hawthorne. Poe's many discussions about tales and his guidelines for those tales provide an excellent foundation for studying the form. Poe also works well for units involving Vonnegut since Poe's works and contributions to literature include the genesis of genre fiction (both detective fiction and science fiction) and arguments about the tensions between popular and literary fiction. The web offers excellent resources for exploring Poe's contributions to short fiction (notably the Wikipedia—http://en.wikipedia.org/wiki/Edgar_Allan_Poe). Students will also, however, need to be directed to Poe's own short stories and his discussion of the tale, particularly *The Philosophy of Composition*.

- As noted earlier, I often have students read Williams's "The Use of Force," since the story is brief and more easily read than Poe's or Hawthorne's works. I usually followed that introductory discussion of the short story with a whole-class analysis of John Gardner's "Redemption." These foundational discussions lead to asking students to read and analyze Vonnegut's "Harrison Bergeron." (I will discuss "Harrison Bergeron" more fully in a later section.)

STUDENT INSIGHT

Yvonne Mason used "Harrison Bergeron" in a gifted English class of eighth graders. Their perspectives as gifted children yielded interesting responses, often revealing much about the assumptions and misconceptions of gifted children who are biologically young yet intellectually advanced:

> I feel as if some people today, believe that we "gifted" children and young adults are taking an unfair advantage, because we are more intelligent than they may have been. Some people try to put handicaps on us by not teaching at our level or intentionally doing things to make us stoop down to another level. An example of this is in the third grade, I was part of the "challenge" program. Every Monday, for the entire day, we (the "gifted" students) would go to a portable and do challenging work. My regular teacher would give us tests when we got back to class, but we only had five minutes to do it. So, instead of having 20–30 minutes to do a test we only had 5 minutes, so our grade would be critically lowered. There are so many handicaps put on us "gifted" students. In "Harrison Bergeron," Hazel states that Harrison "tried to do the best with what God gave him." The best this society would allow him to do was "normal"

because of some people not as smart. . . . I feel that people make conscious decisions to put handicaps on us, in the same way the Handicapper General does.

—*Philip Garner*

But even though I could identify—I hated [the story]. In no human reality would almost every soul submit to the government rule so easily. Too many people would kick and scream and yell—and a war would probably be the outcome of it all. Sure, no one was above average in "Harrison Bergeron," no one fought because everyone was equal. In no possible reality could everyone agree that this was for the best. Although world peace might be a goal, I think the world will fall fighting others on it because people have individuality and can not stand being average, and can not be average. Would you rather live restrained and die naturally? Or would you rather die fighting for who you are and what you stand for?

—*Caitlin Winstead*

Their life is so much more different than ours because they are all equal in almost everyway. First of all they have to wear bags of lead weights around their necks so they can't run faster or do anything athletically better than anyone else. Some even have bird shot padlocked around their necks, some have them around their arms and legs, and some have them all over, it depends on how strong they are or how big they are. We people in the year 2005 don't have to wear any of that stuff because we don't have a United States Handicapper General. We can be better than other people also, like be smarter, be better at a sport, or be better at anything.

—*Jack Wright*

I don't think that this [story] resembles our daily life in the smallest detail. We don't handicap humans for their intelligence. Who would go through all the trouble to attempt to make humans the same when it is instinct to be different? There is no reason for that. Competitions wouldn't be entertaining any more. There can't be a winner or a loser if everyone is equal. That would be like saying that the unsuccessful baseball players can take steroids, while everyone else has to sit at home. If that happens then you really can't call it a competitive sport. . . . Nobody in their right mind would agree to be disfigured. Who would want to look like everybody else anyway? I'll let you ponder that.

—*Robert Landers*

Forcing hindrances on people, consciously or unknowing, holds them back from what they could possibly be. In "Harrison Bergeron," Harrison was described as looking like Halloween and hardware, because of all of his hindrances. That short story relates to my life now, and my past life in school. Especially in elementary school, some students just did grasp the concept of what we were learning. This happened mostly in math. I became infuriated because it held the whole class up, let alone me. It felt much like a hindrance because I would always have to wait and wait until every single person understood the small concept. I would have to bring a book everyday just to keep me busy while everyone else caught up. It even happens this year, in Algebra I Honors. Some people do not understand the homework, so we spend so much time checking over the homework that we only have five minutes left to go over the lesson! I am happy that I am in advanced classes, because everybody is above average and around the same speed as me. The society of today tells people that they need to be skinny, pretty, handsome, etc. They mention nothing about smarts or how well people should do in school. Even if I think I am, I am not normal. Again, I am expected to make excellent grades because I am smart. I feel like blowing up when people do that to me. That is another reason how I know that I am not considered average, or normal. I am gifted.

—*Dylan Djani*

I believe that the people that were handicapped shouldn't be. I think that all people should be treated equally and not created equally. Many people think that competition isn't good. I strongly disagree, I think that competition is what powers the world to do great things. Without competition then we would have no sports. There would be no sense in any sport or any type of competition. This story has made me think about people being made equally.

—*Andrew Tanzey*

The things that happen in this book could never happen in real life. In this book the government makes everyone equal. The government will never be able to have that much control over the people. People called handicappers are sent out by the government to test out how strong, smart, and pretty people are. If someone is really strong then they have to put weights on. If they are really pretty they have to put bags over their face. If they are smart they have to make something so that they can't think. The better they are at something the more extreme their punishment will be. Harrison Bergeron is a very tall, pretty, strong, and smart person. At the end of the book he tears off all of his handicaps and takes over the government. If the things in this book really happened I think someone with the power to would rebel and take over the government.

—*Walt Robinson*

I have been lucky in my life as I haven't had a teacher who kept me, one, from getting ahead, two, who could catch me when I did, or three, didn't already challenge me. That is until seventh grade, my seventh grade literature teacher was the only teacher I ever had who appeared to challenge me, but taught me nothing. She made me feel much like Harrison Bergeron must have felt, she challenged me by giving me ridiculous assignments with deadlines to match and then never coherently spoke of them again. She expected the best, but never taught us what we needed to know except in passing. She spent the class talking on a tangent or teaching speculation, which she wouldn't accept on a test. That is how I feel like Harrison Bergeron.

—*Adam Sturgeon*

The way they live in this story is completely different from how we live. This new way of life has both advantages and disadvantages. You never feel that you have to be better than anyone is or that anyone is better than you are. Things would eventually get extremely boring; you would never be able to show your gifts and talents. You would never be compelled to have more, but the disadvantage is that you are penalized to have more. They have weights, masks, and whatever else necessary to hold people back, unlike now where they award you and show off to everyone that you have gifts, talents, and/or advantages other people don't. I love living the way we do now compared to how they live, people are proud when you succeed and don't try to put you down or hold you back.

—*Allison Satterfield*

The author does a good job of showing how inadequate society is today. Though today and the society in "Harrison Bergeron" are different in many ways, they represent the same problems. Society has rules that don't have any backing. The rules and laws in the story are exaggerated, but they use things in a physical sense instead of mental. Society holds people back with school systems and [unjust] laws, but in the story the author uses physical things like weights and masks. Harrison was held back by a rubber nose and lead balls, and children that are above average today are held back in the same way. During elementary school, about twelve children were pulled out of class for a few hours per week. Though we did work that was more challenging than our everyday work, we were penalized by our regular teacher. When we got back, the teacher would have all the children that didn't go to challenge at her desk getting one on one attention, in addition to having cookies and juice, and an extra-long recess. Also, the challenge students had to do all of our class work for homework that we missed that night, in addition to the original homework. When we asked the teacher about it, she would just say, "You are in challenge, you should be able to handle it." Though we all agreed that this was unfair, it was fourth grade, and what the teacher said was law. Our challenge teacher refused to go over our regular teacher's head, so we had no choice but to do the several hours of homework we should have been allowed to do at school. Our challenge day was Wednesday, a day which most teachers let up on homework because of church. Every week, we would hope our teacher would give us a break, but she never did. We were being penalized for being intelligent, we were in a situation almost identical to Harrison's.

—Anna Holleman

- -

These responses from Mason's students show the assumptions of students about the concepts in literature as well as student assumptions about responding to literature and stories. I have found that Vonnegut's works, in particular, elicit strong responses from students and are thus excellent works to bring into class when we need to see what students believe and feel about the ideas in literature and the forms of literature. Further, we see in these responses how difficult it is for young students—even ones who are gifted—to see the metaphorical truth behind details. Most of these students fail to see that Vonnegut exaggerates conditions that *do* exist and that people *do* tolerate those conditions because the students are trapped in the literal. This phenomenon is one of the greatest challenges we face in English classrooms.

- The most effective part of my short story unit included requiring students to choose a collection of stories by one author to read. That assignment included having students keep journal entries on at least 10 stories and having students write an original critical analysis of one of those stories. Students often chose *Welcome to the Monkey House,* but they also chose and enjoyed J. D. Salinger's *Nine Stories* and collections by science fiction writers, horror writers, and even some literary collections by writers we usually teach as part of the traditional canon—Fitzgerald, Hemingway, Flannery O'Connor, Eudora Welty, Grace Paley, Joyce Carol Oates.

This brief outline of my short story unit depended heavily on the work of Vonnegut, but I feel the basic elements of the process proved to be crucial as well. Students need some exposure to the historical context of the form and some sense of the traditional terminology and conventions of the short story. Next, students need some guided experiences with short stories that both fit those conventions and challenge those conventions. I believe students also benefit from studying works that stretch their linguistic abilities, such as Gardner's story, but they also need works that are more accessible to their reading and analyzing them on their own, such as Vonnegut's works. The final key component of this unit is having students to read complete collections of stories by a single author. I have made similar assignments with poetry and find that students respond well to extended experiences with one author, particularly if we are asking them to develop sophisticated concepts about a literary genre.

Once I have students familiar with the historical context of the American short story and once they have begun to practice their literary analysis skills on the form, I then want them to begin to develop a habit of evaluating stories. In traditional English courses, we often decide *for* students what stories deserve literary analysis and then ask them to analyze. But I feel we need to foster in students an ability to discern value in art of all kinds on their own. Vonnegut's stories certainly offer a wonderful opportunity to evaluate the quality of published stories about which even Vonnegut himself seems critical. To offer students a frame of reference for such judgments, we can use Karon's wrestling with this dilemma along with Vonnegut's own satirical look at literary analysis.

Karon (Boon, 2001), as mentioned above, notes as a Vonnegut critic that he has begun to notice a re-evaluation by critics of the entire canon of Vonnegut's works, but that Vonnegut's short fiction, particularly his stories published primarily for money early in his career, has received the least attention in that re-evaluation. Karon believes that science is a pivotal element of Vonnegut's short fiction and his novels. He argues that when the science falls apart in the novels (such as the punch cards driving the computers in *Player Piano* feeling dated to readers in the twenty-first century), Vonnegut's novels still succeed as art. Karon wonders if those criteria will hold up when applied to the stories. He applies this formula to Vonnegut's "EPICAC," "Fortitude," and "Unready to Wear"—all of which I will discuss in more detail in a later section. If students evaluate Vonnegut's stories by Karon's method, they will in effect be distinguishing between a popular story and a story that has lasting literary merit.

Interestingly, Vonnegut (2005) himself parodies that distinction in his "Here is a lesson in creative writing" from *A Man without a Country*. In this wonderfully comic piece, Vonnegut charts a number of creative works—the story of Cinderella, Kafka's *The Metamorphosis,* and Shakespeare's *Hamlet,* for example. The piece draws on a traditional approach to plot development and satirizes the mechanical nature of New Criticism—both valuable frames of reference for young students considering short fiction. This essay by Vonnegut forces students to explore the value of plot (which appears to be not valuable at all), the value of characterization (which appears to be quite high—an argument offered by John Gardner concerning fiction), and the ultimate value in a work of art (which appears to be difficult to detail for anyone attempting to distinguish between popular fiction and a masterpiece).

The evolution of my short story unit—aided by the works of Vonnegut—has found a much more effective series of goals. Students need historical contexts for the study of a genre, and they need to become familiar with traditional approaches to literary analysis. But we should also move students to a level of evaluation that shifts the responsibility to the student who has yet to develop fully a sense of how mature readers distinguish between popular stories and serious literature. The short story form represents well this distinction in a number of the more respected writers in American literature, including Vonnegut himself.

Becoming a Short Story Writer with Vonnegut

"And let me say at this point that the best creative writing teachers, like the best editors, excel at teaching, not necessarily at writing," Vonnegut offers, much to the delight of most English teachers who have no time or inclination to be professional writers of short stories (Darton, 2001, p. 244). Yet, this is the same man who has written: "You can't teach people to write well. Writing well is something God lets you do or declines to let you do" (Vonnegut, 1974, p. 25). So which is it?

The truth seems to be that Vonnegut does believe teachers of writing can be effective—but that there are creative limits to the impact teachers can have on the quality of writing that any student can produce. We might argue that if we teach writing well, we can foster more than competent writers, but we cannot by the sheer power of teaching produce a Hemingway or an Alice Walker—and certainly not a Vonnegut. But writing talent—whether a student is gifted or lacking—needs some fostering, some skilled teacher of writing. Writing in general is a daunting task, and I have always been fascinated that teachers of very young children believe that they are helping elementary-age children by asking them to write stories. Children writing fiction! To me, this is quite unfair since it requires children to create the content *and* attempt to manage the overwhelming task of composing. That said, let's look in this section how we can help students experiment with writing short stories through the works of Vonnegut, while maintaining a healthy perception of what it is we want students to accomplish with such an assignment.

I am confident in this argument: Teaching a student to write is essentially the same regardless of the genre—essays, fiction, or poetry. Yet, I also believe that each genre has unique challenges for skilled and novice writers. I offer here a process for fostering students as writers of short fiction, but I want to stress that this fiction-writing process is basically the same as fostering students as writers of nonfiction or poetry. The greatest urge we have to set aside is the false assumption that student writers need to begin writing short fiction from a teacher-imposed template after which we can allow the student to experiment. The most effective process for fostering writers of any age and within any genre is to ask students to explore authentic models of the form they will be writing and to create guidelines themselves from those authentic models to be used as they experiment with their own original pieces. This requires students to develop their own rubrics (see Kohn, 2006, for a recent exploration of the negative impact teacher-made rubrics have on student understanding and empowerment).

Students need rich and varied experiences with short stories as grounding for their own story writing; we will discuss here two different types of stories from Vonnegut—"Harrison Bergeron" as a model of his critically acclaimed stories and "The No-Talent Kid" as a model of slick fiction. However, I am convinced that students need to read more of his stories, such as the entire *Welcome to the Monkey House*. Since I am recommending that we avoid the traditional template approach to teaching the short story and to teaching the writing of stories, we must also bring into our classroom authentic discussions of writing fiction from both writers students enjoy and from writers who themselves have experience as teachers of writing fiction (such as Vonnegut, although his attitude toward the practice of teaching fiction writing may seem counter-productive). Here are some excellent options for books about writing to add to this unit:

- My own journey as a young writer-to-be was profoundly affected by the writing of John Gardner and his many wonderful works about becoming a writer of fiction. I have found over the years that bringing his writing about writing into the classroom works wonderfully. His *On Becoming a Novelist*, *The Art of Fiction*, and *On Writers and Writing* are ideal as sources for us as teachers and for the classroom. Many of these works can be used in part to help students to reframe their perceptions of what makes fiction effective and engaging. Gardner works well in the classroom because he focuses most of his discussion on the value of developing characters in fiction (as opposed to developing a plot, which is what students tend to believe is the most important part of writing a story). Additionally, Gardner writes as a writer *and as a teacher*. His works on writing fiction do not simply say "Show, don't tell" (although he does say that, of course); Gardner gives explicit examples of what works in fiction writing and shares with his readers *how* to practice and produce such writing. Although we have to be careful to recognize that Gardner is deeply committed to his view of what makes quality fiction (many people disagree, and students have the right to disagree as well), his meticulous discussions provide ideal platforms from which to discuss short fiction and the writing of fiction.

- Joyce Carol Oates is, like Vonnegut, a masterful artist who has produced a high number of critically well-received and popular works—in a wide range of genres. Her *The Faith of a Writer* is useful in the classroom since it offers a number of essays that can be shared separately with students while discussing the short story as a genre or while they read her own brilliant stories, such as "Where Are You Going?, Where Have You Been?" Students particularly respond well to essays such as "To a Young Writer," "Running and Writing" (which humanizes the writer), "Notes on Failure," and "Inspiration!" While I recommend teachers and students read this entire work, Oates's "Reading as a Writer" is notable since it combines many of the practices and qualities that I have been recommending throughout this discussion. This essay helps students place the writing of short fiction in a rich literary tradition while emphasizing a practice essential to developing as a writer—reading as a writer.
- *Second Words, Negotiating with the Dead: A Writer on Writing,* and *Writing with Intent* by Margaret Atwood should be added to this list as well. As with Gardner and Oates, Atwood's discussion of fiction and writing fiction can be paired with her own excellent works. Students have always responded well to Gardner, Oates, and Atwood in many different English courses of mine. In these three books Atwood offers insight to her own writing and reviews a number of works by other writers, exposing students to the living world of fiction. Atwood discusses "Writing the Male Character," for example, in *Second Words,* and conversations such as these by practicing writers add an authenticity to our classrooms that is often lacking.

Many other essays and books by writers dealing with writing fiction exist, but these have worked for me. Students need to read a great deal of short stories—many by one author and many by the acknowledged masters of the craft—and they need to explore fiction and story writing through works such as those listed here. Finally, however, we need to lead students to opportunities to design their own rubrics for creating and drafting their own original fiction (Kohn, 2006; Wilson, 2006).

Bringing Vonnegut's short fiction into our classrooms as models for students who are writing their own fiction differs from the traditional approach to reading and analyzing short stories in English courses. First, students should become familiar with reading as writers (again, Oates's essay can provide a basis for this practice). This means that students should approach the stories as models for their own writing. We can pair Vonnegut's "Harrison Bergeron" with his

"The No-Talent Kid" in order to design guiding rubrics for students to write their own stories; these guiding rubrics should identify *by choice* what students are attempting to draft for the teacher. For example, students might choose to write a science fiction story, a serious short story story, or a mass-market story, based on their own interests and the discussions that grow from reading these two stories as writers in the classroom and workshop setting.

I recognize that there exists a natural paradox in my asking teachers to leave a great deal of discovering and experimentation in the hands of students while also stating that we *can* teach students to write short stories. That paradox includes that as teachers we must provide some guidelines and even impose some rules while fostering within our students the skills needed for designing their own guiding strategies as writers. Here we are asking students to read and analyze "Harrison Bergeron" and "The No-Talent Kid" as models for their own writing, but we are bringing to the class the wealth of our expertise as teachers and writers. Students need to be told that these two stories have received much different critical response and that Vonnegut himself sees these two stories in different lights. Yet, in Vonnegut's serious fiction and his mass market fiction, students can cull some guiding questions that will provide them with structure as they attempt to write stories. First, let's look at some Big Picture questions students should explore:

- How can we justify distinguishing between serious fiction and mass market fiction?
- How do Vonnegut's stories conform to broad genre identifications such as "science fiction"?
- Short stories are often judged on their effectiveness to engage the reader quickly, usually within the first paragraph or even the first sentence. How do Vonnegut's stories succeed in compelling the reader to continue reading?
- Most writers value character development over plot development. How does Vonnegut create engaging and memorable characters in his stories? Further, some critics have argued that Vonnegut's characters are two-dimensional, thus weak. Do you see Vonnegut's characters as well developed? Do you see his character development as a strength or a weakness?
- Another key element in short stories is tone. Vonnegut often weaves both humorous and deeply serious tones and topics throughout his works. How does Vonnegut create tone in his stories? What makes Vonnegut's varying tones effective?
- Does Vonnegut conform to the traditional expectations for plot development in his stories? Does he achieve a satisfying conclusion to his stories? How does he manage plot?

A student-centered and discovery approach to having students write short stories does not remove the expertise of the teacher from the lessons—as you can see from the above guiding questions. But the teacher's role becomes one where the teacher asks questions that include the content students need as they develop their own level of expertise. We are trying to create a writing workshop atmosphere that is targeted on the writing of fiction. Students must have, then, ample time to read and discuss the two stories, keeping their focus on reading as writers. They must also have ample time to experiment with their writing process as it concerns fiction writing. *Many writers discover that they have different writing processes for different writing purposes.* Students must be given the opportunity to discover this and to refine that process as they write fiction on demand. Vonnegut writes explicitly about drawing out elaborate charts for the drafting of *Slaughterhouse-Five* just as many of the writers mentioned in this section explain how their fiction grows from an idea to a story. If we want students to have authentic experiences with writing stories, they will need adequate time in class to draft their stories and to experiment with their own lives as writers.

Reading, learning, and teaching "Harrison Bergeron" along with "The No-Talent Kid" can fill a literature unit without considering these stories as an avenue to writing short stories. Since "Harrison Bergeron" stands as a commonly taught Vonnegut piece, I will outline here briefly some elements of dealing with these two stories offering how they fit into having students write short stories and adding some broader issues if you wish to teach these stories as a traditional unit on short fiction:

- "Harrison Bergeron" and "The No-Talent Kid" are excellent examples of the unique demands of paragraphing and managing dialogue in fiction. While paragraphing and dialogue can be key features and concerns of many genres, they certainly have conventional standards in short stories that novice writers should address. Despite Vonnegut's reputation as experimental and postmodern, his stories are highly conventional in terms of dialogue. Once we establish for students the mechanics of formatting and managing dialogue (how we place quote marks and punctuation with quote marks or the convention of starting new paragraphs with each new speaker, for example), we can begin to ask students how writers capture the rhythms of the spoken word—particularly as those patterns help develop the characters (do teens talk differently than their teachers, for example?)—and to challenge students to compose dialogue that avoids sounding artificial and orchestrated although, by its nature, all dialogue in fiction is artificial.

- These stories in distinct ways deal with politics. "Harrison Bergeron" addresses universal concerns about the potentially oppressive nature of government while "The No-Talent Kid" dramatizes the politics of student-teacher or child-adult relationships. Both stories address the locus of power in human interaction. For our students who are experimenting as writers, these stories are ripe for preaching the most central mantra of fiction writing—show, don't tell. Vonnegut would be much less effective and his writing would be much less enjoyable if he simply wrote, "Watch out! Governments can be oppressive," or "OK, kids, to be an adult you have to learn how to negotiate from a position of strength, not a position of weakness." The stories themselves are much more dynamic than these quasi-thematic statements. And that is what skilled writers of fiction do; they show.
- We are reading and studying these stories under the assumption that "Harrison Bergeron" is of greater literary merit than "The No-Talent Kid." While this concept is a complex one, we should look for opportunities to help students begin to establish for themselves how our culture distinguishes between the merely popular and the artistic. No simple formula exists, of course, and many people disagree on where to place many creative works (including the works of Vonnegut). Yet, having some basis for making this distinction will be valuable to our students as they analyze literature and write themselves. In these two stories, students are often able to see that Vonnegut deals with *tension* differently. "Harrison Bergeron" certainly builds tension in the reader over the conflict between Harrison and the oppressive government. That tension is developed through the eyes of his parents, and it is tinted with contrasting degrees of humor and danger. The short story form tends to create a "neat" package in that things work out in some way by the end of a relatively brief story, and such is the case with the shooting of Harrison. What often distinguishes more sophisticated stories from slick stories, however, is the degree of the cleverness of such conclusions. "The No-Talent Kid" is a story that works out with a precision and cleverness that distinguishes it from "Harrison Bergeron." For students, these stories are excellent examples of how we argue over the quality of fictional tension and the quality of endings to stories that end in ways that satisfy the reader without being too pat, too easy to predict.

Vonnegut's Stories—Artificial Intelligence, Ironic Science, and Free Will

Karon (Boon, 2001) explains that Vonnegut's short stories have been ignored, "denigrated," and gradually acknowledged as valuable documents if we want to explore the development of Vonnegut as a writer and as a novelist (pp. 105–106). He does concede that he believes more critics will begin to embrace many of Vonnegut's stories as valuable in themselves, and I agree. I believe we can bring Vonnegut's stories into our classrooms paired with classic works in the genre by Hemingway, O'Connor, and Poe—among many others. Karon offers an interesting argument for determining which stories we should embrace by Vonnegut; he argues that if we examine how science works or fails in Vonnegut's stories we can uncover a clue to the value in his stories. Using Karon's premise, I will discuss here how we can bring several of Vonnegut's stories—"EPICAC," "Unready to Wear," "Fortitude"—to our study of short stories

ENTRY POINTS

Many of the stories discussed here involve artificial intelligence or preserving human intelligence beyond the normal life span; these are certainly popular topics in science fiction. Many movies deal wonderfully with these ideas, and many prove to be excellent entry points into Vonnegut's stories—depending on the age and maturity level of the classes. *2001: A Space Odyssey* and *The Man with Two Brains* are excellent movies for this unit. *2001*, of course, is a modern classic in the science fiction genre for both movies and novels. The computer, Hal, is unforgettable in the movie. (Web pages exist, in fact, that have links to sound bites from Hal's more famous lines in the movie.) A much less serious look at preserving human intelligence beyond our corporeal lives is Steve Martin's *The Man with Two Brains*. This overlooked movie fits well with Vonnegut because humor is juxtaposed with some truly dark motifs running through the movie. Showing brief clips from either movie would work well also.

CONNECTION

The ideal novel connection with this unit is Mary Shelley's *Frankenstein*. The novel has spawned many movie versions as well. When paired with Vonnegut, this classic work is fertile ground for debating the characteristics of science fiction. Students might be less inclined to identify an older work as science fiction since they do not readily associate the nineteenth century with modern science.

"EPICAC" and "Unready to Wear" are included in Vonnegut's *Welcome to the Monkey House*, and "Fortitude" can be found in *Wampeters, Foma & Granfalloons*. "EPICAC" is Vonnegut's exploration of artificial intelligence (making it ideal to pair with *2001*); "Unready to Wear" deals with evolution (thus a natural connection with Vonnegut's *Galapagos*); and "Fortitude"—although it seems to be a play—is a short story about maintaining human intelligence beyond the normal boundaries of the life of a fully intact body (something of a *Frankenstein* exploration; there is even a character with that name). Karon (Boon, 2001) argues that these stories are excellent examples of why we should hold Vonnegut's short fiction in higher regard. He believes that these works succeed regardless of how valid the science is within the works; other stories by Vonnegut fail along with the science, however.

"EPICAC" reminds me in many ways of *Player Piano* since the science involved is both highly relevant today in terms of the issues (artificial intelligence in the short story and corporate use—and misuse—of science in the novel) while both are simultaneously flawed when contemporary readers compare the science in the stories with how that same science looks today. Yet, as Karon (Boon, 2001) notes, the story works because it is Vonnegut's questions *about* the larger concerns of science in the story that matter—not the details of how the science looks in the real world: "Using science in an ironic manner—as Vonnegut often does in his novels and sometimes does in his short stories—helps us probe what we are and what we should do, the traditional concerns of philosophy. Irony always is a sort of questioning, and no one questions better than Vonnegut does" (p. 111). "EPICAC," then, as part of a study of the short story offers these discussions:

- What is the nature of human intelligence? And can that be captured by a computer?
- What constitutes a conversation?
- What makes a being human? And what roles do intelligence and emotion play in that dynamic?

If Karon's argument about the use of "ironic science" in Vonnegut's short stories is accurate (and I think it is), we seem to be left as readers and teachers with helping our students see that science in Vonnegut is a device for raising enduring questions through fiction. "Fortitude" does such as well as "EPICAC" except that "Fortitude" addresses human nature and human intelligence—whether or not each of those qualities is bound by our corporeal form. The form of this story is also interesting for class discussions since it appears to be a play. Just as Steve Martin plays with animating the human brain in the movie mentioned above, Vonnegut's story deals with Sylvia, who had the fortitude to exist as just a head, surviving seventy-eight operations over thirty-six years! Where "EPICAC" examines the possibility of artificial versions of human intelligence, "Fortitude" "questions at what point we lose our personhood," explains Karon (Boon, 2001, p. 111).

CONNECTION

Vonnegut's science brings his readers to philosophical concerns about life and living—and, naturally, about death and suicide. Students may find discussions of life, death, and suicide challenging, and high school and college years tend to be the times when young people do confront those ideas. A brief and effective piece dealing with the human condition and the fact that being human is directly linked with our ability to take our own lives is Albert Camus's essay, "The Myth of Sisyphus." Camus also wrote many other brief pieces that deal with suicide and the human condition, but this famous essay can be used effectively to introduce students to modern existential philosophy, absurdist motifs, and the reframing of classic myths in modern terms. Many of the qualities found in Camus provide students with firm groundings for addressing those same qualities in Vonnegut's fiction.

If we pair "EPICAC" with "Fortitude," students can be asked to debate the issue of life and death as it is addressed differently in the two stories: "Though the technical details of Sylvia's machine-human fusion are as sketchy as EPICAC's, EPICAC *could* kill himself," adds Karon (Boon, 2001, p. 111). We are asked to set aside the science of either EPICAC's or Sylvia's humanity in order to wrestle with the nature of living, the quality of life, and the ultimate morality of taking one's own life. Running through these heavy and serious issues, as well, are Vonnegut's irony and humor—qualities that challenge high school and college students as much as the topics do.

These two stories seem to suggest that our bodies and our emotions are sources of human suffering; thus, without the body, humans have some chance at happiness (Boon, 2001). Predating by thirty years *Galapagos,* "Unready to Wear" carries evolutionary thought to the conclusion suggested in "EPICAC" and "Fortitude"—the future of humanity does not include the body. "Unready to Wear" adds another dimension to what students consider as "science." Often, we view science as technology, but science also is a way to explain the universe. Evolutionary theory is a scientific explanation for how humans have become *human.* As I have noted in an earlier chapter, the debates surrounding evolutionary theory remain contentious—suggesting that we need to address those tensions as often as possible so that our students do not fall prey to false arguments. "Unready to Wear" allows us a perfect setting for discussing how humans evolve (and how satisfied we are with science's explanation for that evolution) without impinging on the sanctity of the science classroom—where philosophical and religious concerns genuinely have little or no place.

By adding Vonnegut's short fiction to our classes, we expose students to the philosophical questions that are universal—even though the details of Vonnegut's science in his fiction is often flawed and dated. Do humans have free will and is that free will part of what makes humans *human*? And how should we deal with that free will when it involves our ability to take our own lives? These questions are raised by the ironic science of Vonnegut's stories that confront artificial intelligence, the nature of human intelligence, and the future of human evolution—while addressing these issues with both deep seriousness and cutting humor.

ENTRY POINTS AND CONNECTIONS

"The Use of Force," William Carlos Williams

2001: A Space Odyssey

The Man with Two Brains

Frankenstein, Mary Shelley

"The Myth of Sisyphus," Albert Camus

Conclusion: Reading, Learning, Teaching Kurt Vonnegut

Vonnegut as narrator of *Breakfast of Champions* claims that he is transformed by his own creation, the character Rabo Karabekian who returns to the pages of a Vonnegut novel in *Bluebeard*. I am now completing a book about the writer who I would claim has transformed me—and who continues to transform me each time I read something new or reread something treasured by him.

When I began the last half of Chapter Six dealing with *Breakfast of Champions,* I could not resist rereading that novel in its entirety; I did so in two days and for, well, I have no idea how many times. It is possibly the novel I have read most often in my life. However, rereading it was as if I had never read the novel. Of course, I am who I have never been before, older and reading the novel as a person writing about it. I am offering these thoughts because I am experiencing something akin to buyer's remorse—except this is writer's remorse.

Why?

Because there is a part of me who wishes that Vonnegut would stay outside the traditional setting of the English classroom, forever a novelist that young people discover and read *in spite* of adults. A novel that young people read as a thumbing of their noses at all things adult.

But I will deliver this book to my publisher and I hope it finds its ways into the hands of teachers and readers who feel the same affection I do for Vonnegut and what he has to say to all of humanity.

I cannot end this book with anything better than what Vonnegut has offered himself in *Palm Sunday:*

Laughter and tears are both responses to frustration and exhaustion, to the futility of thinking and striving anymore. I myself prefer to laugh, since there is less cleaning up to do afterward—and since I can start thinking and striving again that much sooner. (p. 298)

• • •

So it goes . . .

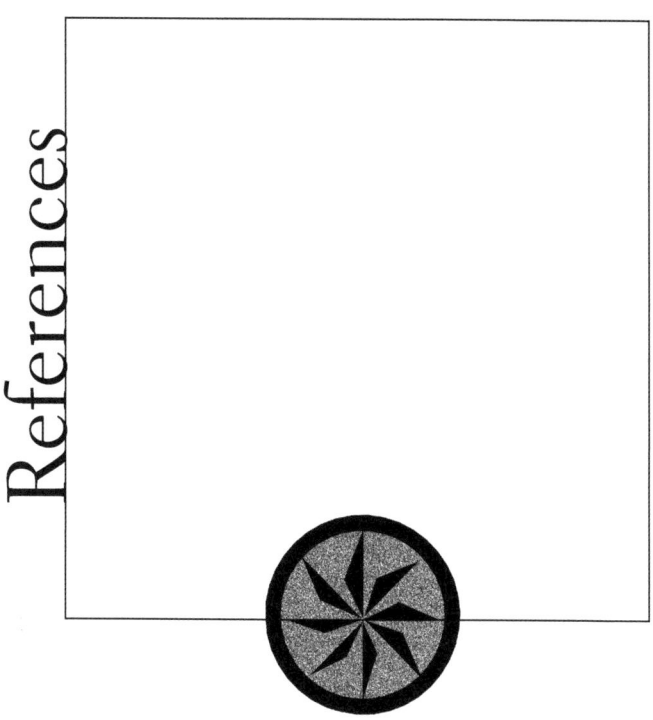

References

Allen, W. (1980). *Side effects.* New York: Ballantine Books.

Allen, W. R. (1988). *Conversations with Kurt Vonnegut.* Jackson: University Press of Mississippi.

Allen, W. R. (1991). *Understanding Kurt Vonnegut.* Columbia: University of South Carolina Press.

Atwood, M. (2005). *Writing with intent: Essays, reviews, personal prose: 1983–2005.* New York: Carroll and Graf Publishers.

Barris, C. (2002). *Confessions of a dangerous mind: An unauthorized autobiography.* New York: Miramax Books.

Bloom, H. (1994). *The western canon: The books and school of the ages.* New York: Harcourt, Brace and Company.

Boon, K. A., ed. (2001). *At millennium's end: New essays on the work of Kurt Vonnegut.* Albany, NY: State University of New York Press.

Campbell, J., & Moyers, B. (1988). *The power of myth.* New York: Doubleday.

Confessions of a Dangerous Mind. (2003). Dir. George Clooney. Miramax Films.

Darton, J. (2001). *Writers on writing: Collected essays from* The New York Times. New York: Times Books.

Freire, P. (1993). *Pedagogy of the oppressed.* New York: Continuum.

Frost, R. (1969). *The poetry of Robert Frost: The collected poems, complete and unabridged.* New York: Henry Holt and Company.

Gardner, H. (2000). *The disciplined mind: Beyond facts and standardized tests, the K-12 education that every child deserves.* New York: Penguin.

REFERENCES

Gardner, J. (1991). *The art of fiction: Notes on craft for young writers.* New York: Vintage Books.

Gardner, J. (1999). *On becoming a novelist.* New York: W. W. Norton, and Co.

Gardner, J. (1978). *On moral fiction.* New York: Basic Books, Inc.

Greene, M. (1995). *Releasing the imagination: Essays on education, the arts, and social change.* San Francisco: Jossey-Bass.

Hedges, W. (1997). New Criticism explained. Available online at: http://www.sou.edu/English/Hedges/Sodashop/RCenter/Theory/Explaind/ncritexp.htm.

Huber, C. (2005). The Vonnegut web. Available online at: http://www.vonnegutweb.com/index.html.

Jacoby, S. (2004). *Freethinkers: A history of American secularism.* New York: Metropolitan Books.

Kafka, F. (1979). *The basic Kafka.* New York: Pocket.

Kingsolver, B. (1998). *Another America: Otra America.* Trans. Rebecca Cartes. New York: Seal.

Klinkowitz, J. (1990). Slaughterhouse-Five: *Reforming the novel and the world.* Boston: Twayne Publishers.

Klinkowitz, J. (1998). *Vonnegut in fact: The public spokesmanship of personal fiction.* Columbia: University of South Carolina Press.

Kohn, A. (2006, March). The trouble with rubrics. *English Journal, 95* (4), 12–15.

Marek Vit's Kurt Vonnegut Corner. (2002). Available online at: http://www.geocities.com/Hollywood/4953/vonn.html.

Marvin, T. F. (2002). *Kurt Vonnegut: A critical companion.* Westport, CT: Greenwood Press.

Merrill, R., ed. (1990). *Critical essays on Kurt Vonnegut.* Boston: G. K. Hall and Company.

Morse, D. E. (2003). *The novels of Kurt Vonnegut: Imagining being an American.* Westport, CT: Praeger.

Mustazza, L. (1990). *Forever pursuing genesis: The myth of Eden in the novels of Kurt Vonnegut.* Lewisberg: Bucknell University Press.

Mustazza, L., ed. (1994). *The critical response to Kurt Vonnegut.* Westport, CT: Greenwood Press.

Nabokov, V. (1989). *Lolita.* New York: Vintage.

The New Oxford Annotated Bible. (1991). New York: Oxford University Press.

Oates, J. C. (1992). *Black water.* New York: Dutton.

The Official Website of Kurt Vonnegut. (2002). Available online at: http://www.vonnegut.com.

Orwell, G. (1968). *In front of your nose, 1945–1950 (The collected essays, journalism and letters of George Orwell)*. Eds. S. Orwell & I. Angus. New York: Harcourt, Brace and World, Inc.

Paley, G. (1994). *The collected stories*. New York: Farrar Straus Giroux.

Pawel, E. (1984). *The nightmare of reason*. New York: Farrar, Straus, and Giroux.

Reed, P. J., & Leeds, M., eds. (1996). *The Vonnegut chronicles: Interviews and essays*. Westport, CT: Greenwood Press.

Rosenblatt, L. (1995). *Literature as exploration*. 5th ed. New York: The Modern Language Association of America.

Schatt, S. (1976). *Kurt Vonnegut*. Boston: Twayne Publishers.

Scheele, A. (2004, May 6). The good student trap. *Washington Post*. Retrieved May 10, 2004, from: http://www.washingtonpost.com

Thomas, P. L. (2004). *Numbers games: Measuring and mandating American education*. New York: Peter Lang.

Thomas, P. L. (2005a). *Reading, learning, teaching Barbara Kingsolver*. New York: Peter Lang.

Thomas, P. L. (2005b). *Teaching writing primer*. New York: Peter Lang.

Thomas, P. L., & Welchel, E. (2005). The art *from* war—American classrooms and literary responses to war. *Oregon English Journal, 27* (1), 26–29.

Twain, M. (1981). *The adventures of Huckleberry Finn*. New York: Bantam Books.

Vonnegut, K. (1999a). *Bagombo snuff box: Uncollected short fiction*. New York: G. P. Putnam's Sons.

Vonnegut, K. (1987). *Bluebeard*. New York: Delta.

Vonnegut, K. (1973). *Breakfast of champions or goodbye blue Monday!*. New York: Delta.

Vonnegut, K. (1963). *Cat's cradle*. New York: Delta.

Vonnegut, K. (1982). *Deadeye Dick*. New York: Delta.

Vonnegut, K. (1991). *Fates worse than death*. New York: Delta.

Vonnegut, K. (1985). *Galapagos*. New York: Delta.

Vonnegut, K. (1999b). *God bless you, Dr. Kevorkian*. New York: Seven Stories Press.

Vonnegut, K. (1965). *God bless you, Mr. Rosewater*. New York: Delta.

Vonnegut, K. (1971/1978). *Happy birthday, Wanda June*. New York: Delta.

Vonnegut, K. (1990). *Hocus pocus*. New York: Berkley Books.

Vonnegut, K. (1979). *Jailbird*. New York: Delta.

Vonnegut, K. (2005). *A man without a country*. New York: Seven Stories Press.

Vonnegut, K. (1961/1966). *Mother night*. New York: Delta.

Vonnegut, K. (1981). *Palm Sunday*. New York: Delta.

REFERENCES

Vonnegut, K. (1952/1980). *Player piano.* New York: Delta.

Vonnegut, K. (1959). *The sirens of Titan.* New York: Delta.

Vonnegut, K. (1976). *Slapstick or lonesome no more!.* New York: Delta.

Vonnegut, K. (1969). *Slaughterhouse-five or the children's crusade: A duty-dance with death.* New York: Delta.

Vonnegut, K. (1997). *Timequake.* New York: G. P. Putnam's Sons.

Vonnegut, K. (1974). *Wampeters, foma & granfalloons.* New York: Delta.

Vonnegut, K. (1968). *Welcome to the monkey house.* New York: Delta.

Weaver, C. (1996). *Teaching grammar in context.* Portsmouth, NH: Boynton/Cook Publishers.

Wilson, M. (2006). *Rethinking rubrics in writing assessment.* Portsmouth, NH: Heinemann.

Zinn, H. (1995). *A people's history of the United States: 1492-present.* Rev. and updated ed. New York: Harper Perennial.

Zinsser, W. (2001). *On writing well: The classic guide to writing nonfiction.* 25th Anniversary Ed. New York: Quill/ A Harper Resource Book.

Confronting the Text, Confronting the World
Bringing Writers into the Classroom

This series in Peter Lang's education list features volumes that focus on one writer whose works are suitable for English classrooms at the high school and college levels. These books are a blend of introductions to the authors and their works, critical interpretation, explorations of best practice in reading and writing, and provocative considerations of learning theory and pedagogy.

Volumes explore authors such as:
- Barbara Kingsolver
- Kurt Vonnegut
- Howard Zinn
- Margaret Atwood
- Toni Morrison
- Ralph Ellison
- Clyde Edgerton
- James Dickey

To order other books in this series, please contact our Customer Service Department:

(800) 770-LANG (within the U.S.)
(212) 647-7706 (outside the U.S.)
(212) 647-7707 FAX

Or browse online by series:
www.peterlang.com